Singapore's
Foreign Policy

The Search for Regional Order

Singapore's Foreign Policy

The Search for Regional Order

Amitav Acharya
University of Bristol, UK

Institute of
Policy Studies

World Scientific

NEW JERSEY · LONDON · SINGAPORE · BEIJING · SHANGHAI · HONG KONG · TAIPEI · CHENNAI

Published by

World Scientific Publishing Co. Pte. Ltd.

5 Toh Tuck Link, Singapore 596224

USA office: 27 Warren Street, Suite 401-402, Hackensack, NJ 07601

UK office: 57 Shelton Street, Covent Garden, London WC2H 9HE

Library of Congress Cataloging-in-Publication Data
Acharya, Amitav.
    Singapore's foreign policy : the search for regional order / by Amitav Acharya.
    p. cm.
    Includes bibliographical references and index.
    ISBN-13: 978-981-270-859-5
    ISBN-10: 981-270-859-6
    ISBN-13: 978-981-277-888-8 (pbk)
    ISBN-10: 981-277-888-8 (pbk)
    1. Singapore--Foreign relations. I. Title.
    DS610.45.A35 2007
    327.5957--dc22

                                                            2007042804

British Library Cataloguing-in-Publication Data
A catalogue record for this book is available from the British Library.

Cover photograph: Provided by the ASEAN Secretariat, Jakarta.

Typeset by Stallion Press
Email: enquiries@stallionpress.com

Printed by Fulsland Offset Printing (S) Pte Ltd, Singapore

Preface

This book presents essays on Singapore's foreign and national security policy that were written in two different periods: early 1990s and early 2000s — an interval of 8–10 years. Readers will notice that this is not a systematic or comprehensive survey of Singapore's foreign policy; nor does it have strict historic continuity between the above two periods. Nevertheless, I decided to put these essays together mainly because, taken together, they highlight the need for moving beyond the traditional realist perspective on Singapore's foreign policy. Moreover, Chapter 1, entitled "The Evolution of Singapore's Foreign Policy", had remained unpublished after being presented at a conference at the University of Windsor in Canada in 1992, and I felt the argument of this essay deserved to be brought to the attention of contemporary students and observers of Singapore's foreign policy.

Professor Garry Rodan invited me to speak at a conference on Singapore at Murdoch University in Perth in 1992, and thus got me started on the essay on Singapore's foreign and national security policy. But without M. Ramesh's help and involvement as co-author, this essay could not have been completed.

The idea of bringing all these essays into a book actually owes its inspiration to the several invitations I received from the annual *Singapore Perspectives* conference organized by the Institute of Policy Studies (IPS). Chapters 3, 4 and 5 were thus written for the IPS Conferences in 2002, 2004 and 2006. I am indebted to IPS' chairman, Professor Tommy Koh, and its Deputy and Acting Director,

Arun Mahizhnan, for inviting an outsider to analyze Singapore's foreign policy for a largely domestic audience.

Herbert Lin, now pursuing his doctorate at the University of Chicago, helped to arrange the chapters in some order and created the bibliography. My publisher, World Scientific, deserves special thanks for accepting the manuscript, and Yvonne Tan for editorial work on the book. June Abad of the ASEAN Secretariat dug up the cover photo from the ASEAN archives.

Although this is a book about foreign policy, it is closely woven around Singapore's national security concerns and approach as well. I have not changed the tense or the language of the chapters, except for minor editorial purposes. The documentary appendices have been selected for their relevance to the main arguments of the book; they do not represent a comprehensive list of documents on Singapore's foreign policy.

Contents

Introduction

Rethinking Singapore's Foreign Policy

The conventional understanding of Singapore's foreign policy can be summed up in three main propositions. First, it is dictated by the imperatives of a small state, which Singapore undoubtedly is, at least in a physical sense. Second, and closely following from the above, the primary purpose of Singapore's foreign policy is to ensure its survival. Third, this logic of survival supports a realist understanding of international relations and dictates a *realpolitik* approach to foreign policy and national security. As Michael Leifer, in his widely known book on Singapore's foreign policy, wrote, "Singapore's leaders have consistently approached the matter of foreign policy from the conventional realist perspective of a small state obliged to cope with a world that was potentially hostile and without common government."[1] This implies, among other things, reliance on a strong national defense capability, an emphasis on unilateralism and bilateralism over regionalism and multilateralism, a preference for US military presence to maintain the regional balance of power and a consequent prioritization of international engagement in which defense and strategic relations with external powers assumes salience over regional ties or commitment to regionalism or closer identification with its neighbors.

This collection of essays, written over a period of 13 years (between 1992 and 2005), is intended not as a systematic and

---

[1] Michael Leifer, *Singapore's Foreign Policy: Coping with Vulnerability*, London, Routledge, 2000.

comprehensive record of Singapore's foreign policy. Rather, its purpose is to provide an alternative interpretation and argument about the underpinnings and directions of Singapore's foreign policy.

The main argument of these essays, supported by a selection of documents that highlight the mixed strategies underlying Singapore's foreign policy, is that Singapore's foreign policy approach cannot be understood solely in terms of the above tenets of realism and *realpolitik*. Alternative conceptions of international relations, including liberal institutionalism and social constructivism,[2] offer valuable insights into how the Republic's foreign policy has evolved and must be taken seriously by anyone who wants to investigate how Singapore has not only ensured its survival, but also "punched above its weight", to use a cliché, at the regional and international level.

Realism as a theory of international relations, associated with the work of Thucidydes, Machiavelli, Hobbes, E.H. Carr, Morgenthau and Kissinger, makes the following assumptions:

(1) states are the main units of international relations and anarchy, defined as the absence of any higher form of authority above the state, is the basic feature of the international system;

(2) the main goal of states is to ensure their survival and pursue their national interest (both of which may require them to seek greater power relative to their neighbors);

(3) as a consequence, conflict and war becomes a natural order of things and are almost inevitable;

---

[2] An attempt to go beyond realism by invoking interdependence theory is N. Ganesan, *Realism and Interdependence in Singapore's Foreign Policy*, London, Routledge, 2005. For comparative analyses of realism, liberal institutionalism and constructivism as theoretical approaches to the international relations of Southeast Asian states, see: Amitav Acharya, "Realism, Institutionalism and the Asian Economic Crisis", *Contemporary Southeast Asia*, vol. 21, no. 1, 1999, pp. 1–29; Amitav Acharya, "Do Norms and Identity Matter? Community and Power in Southeast Asia's Regional Order", *Pacific Review*, vol. 18, no. 1, 2005, pp. 95–118; Nikolas Busse, "Constructivism and Southeast Asian Security", *Pacific Review*, vol. 12, no. 1, 1999, pp. 39–60; Sorpong Peou, "Realism and Constructivism in Southeast Asian Security Studies Today", *Pacific Review*, vol. 15, no. 1, 2002, pp. 1–20.

(4) international relations is a zero-sum game in which states are more concerned with their relative gains ("how much you win, how much I win", rather than win-win solutions);

(5) international institutions have only a marginal effect in promoting peace and cooperation; and

(6) the key to international order is balance of power, defined primarily in economic and military terms. By comparison, economic interdependence and international institutions are of little value as mechanisms for maintaining order in international relations; interdependence may actually act as a cause of conflict.

While the foreign policy statements of Singapore's leaders (especially its founders, as discussed in Chapter 1) suggest a stark realist view of international relations consistent with the above propositions, the country's actual foreign policy strategy and behavior point to a much more complex picture. To understand these more complex underpinnings of Singapore's foreign policy, liberal institutionalist and social constructivist understandings of international relations are especially helpful correctives to conventional realist analysis.

Liberal institutionalism holds that international institutions — broadly defined to include regimes and formal organizations — regulate and constrain state preferences by, among other things, developing norms of conduct, facilitating information-sharing, reducing transaction costs and maximizing the payoffs of interdependence. Classical liberalism, associated with Immanuel Kant, John Stuart Mill and Woodrow Wilson, rested on three pillars: commercial liberalism, or the view that economic interdependence, especially free trade, reduces the prospect of war and the utility of force; (2) republican liberalism, or the "democratic peace" argument which assumes that liberal democracies are more peaceful than autocracies or at least seldom fight one another; and (3) the institutionalist argument, which focuses on the contribution of international organizations in managing conflict and promoting cooperation. Some liberals, such as the adherents to what has been called neo-liberal institutionalism, accept international anarchy as a basic feature of world politics, but challenge realism by arguing in favor of the role of institutions in moderating the condition of anarchy and promoting peace. Those seeking to understand how Singapore's foreign policy has evolved may benefit as much, if not more, by paying attention to the first and third of these liberal mechanisms as by using the realist framework that discounts the pacific effects of both economic interdependence and international institutions.

Another helpful perspective in understanding Singapore's foreign policy is social constructivism, which holds that the national interests and identities of states are not given, but socially constructed through their mutual interactions. International relations are shaped not just by material forces such as military power and wealth, but also by norms, identity-building and common values. International norms such as non-intervention and pacific settlement of disputes, once established, have a life of their own; they create and redefine state interests and approaches. Constructivists take international relations as a social process, rather than as a "strategic interaction". Conditions such as anarchy and power politics are not permanent or "organic" features of international relations. Even under conditions of anarchy (the absence of a higher authority above the state), states lead a social life. International multilateral and regional institutions act as vital mediums for such socialization. Through interaction and socialization, states may develop a "collective identity" that would enable them to overcome power politics and the security dilemma.

The essays in this book offer four main reasons to challenge the conventional realist understanding of Singapore's foreign policy and call for introducing alternative understandings such as those offered by liberal institutionalism and social constructivism.

First, it neglects the strong underpinnings of Singapore's economic and security policy in liberal market economics. In fact, the most famous books on Singapore's foreign policy have paid little attention to the economic underpinnings of its national security. As Chapter 2 of this book (and the speech by Foreign Minister S. Rajaratnam entitled "Singapore: Global City", included in the Appendix) demonstrates, Singapore's foreign economic policy and its national security approach, in the broader sense of the term, is dictated by the liberal framework of globalization rather than the mercantilist notion of self-reliance and autarchy, which would be closer to realism. As a pioneering state which used globalization to its advantage well before the term became popular in international discourse, Singapore also has to allow the liberal underpinnings of the global market economy in devising its foreign policy.

Second, realists vastly overstate the balance of power approach to regional order in Singapore's foreign policy at the expense of the multilateralist and regionalist approach. Singapore's close identification with the US security strategy in the region, based on the belief that the US is the indispensable regional balancer, is a fact. Singapore's policy-makers, despite extoling the beneficial effects of the US military presence, are also acutely aware of the potential and actual costs of security dependence it engenders. They have shunned the status of becoming a formal American ally. As Chapters 3 and 4 show, Singapore is a close ally of the US in the war on terror and a member of the "coalition of the willing" over Iraq. But upon closer reflection, this appears to have been due more to the Bush administration's open hostility to even minor forms of dissent from its preemptive strategy and its strike on Iraq, than to a shared understanding of the sources of terrorism or approaches to combat the menace.

A third argument against the conventional view is that it seriously understates the impact of ASEAN in realizing Singapore's vital foreign policy and security interests, including the preservation of its sovereignty and territorial integrity. Few accounts of Singapore's foreign policy have seriously wondered how, without the regionalist turn in Indonesia's foreign policy under Suharto, would Singapore have managed its security at a time of British withdrawal from the east of Suez, the US preoccupation in Vietnam and the Nixon Doctrine's stipulation regarding avoiding further direct military intervention in Asia, especially at a time when Singapore's own self-defense forces were too miniscule to provide credible deterrence. Singapore's reliance on ASEAN for ensuring its sovereignty *vis-à-vis* its larger and more powerful neighbors, through the principle of non-intervention and non-use-of-force which ASEAN so strenuously championed, is much more consistent with the tenets of neo-liberal institutionalism than realism.

Moreover, Singapore's foreign policy-makers have not found it difficult to reconcile their national interests with regional cooperation. Chapter 1 points out how regionalism has increasingly crept into and moderated the initially crude and severe *realpolitik* worldview of Singapore's founding leaders. Chapter 3 shows the variety of ways in which Singapore's leaders, when facing hard times induced by the lingering fallout of the Asian financial crisis of 1997, continued their engagement with existing regional institutions such as ASEAN, Asia-Pacific Economic Cooperation (APEC) and ASEAN Regional Forum (ARF), while at the same time helping to formulate new forms of regionalism and inter-regionalism, including the ASEAN Plus Three (APT) and East Asia–Latin America Cooperation (EALAC). Later, Singapore would host the first Asia–Middle East Dialogue. In a similar vein, Chapter 5 discusses how Singapore spoke the need for an ASEAN identity as a way of coping with the simultaneous rise of China and India. The setting for this apparent synthesis between regionalism and *realpolitik* comes from the nature of ASEAN regionalism itself, which at its origin was not intended to replicate West European supranationalism, but to serve as the framework through which member states can pursue their national interests in a manner consistent with the interests of their neighbors. This role of ASEAN was not lost on Singapore's foreign policy-makers, so much so that one of them, former Foreign Minister Wong Kan Seng, in his contribution to *The Little Red Dot*, described ASEAN as one of three elements of Singapore's vital interests. This relates to the social constructivist understanding of international relations: interests and identities of states are neither a given nor do they remain constant, but emerge and change through a process of mutual interactions and socialization, and states define their national interest only through a process of mutual interactions. When states begin to see international cooperation and institutions as integral to their vital interests and when they define their national interests by including these institutions, then the resulting dynamic supports a more liberal and social constructivist view of international relations than the realist view.

Fourth, the conventional view also understates the significance of Singapore's role in global multilateral forums and especially in the development of regionalism in Southeast Asia. Belying the standard realist pessimism about the relevance and effectiveness of international institutions, Singapore has produced some of the ablest multilateralists in its diplomatic corps, as evident in Tommy Koh's stewardship of the UN Law of the Sea Conference and the UN Conference on Environment and Development in Rio. Yet, this apparent paradox is hardly surprising when one considers the essentially liberal globalist underpinnings of Singapore's foreign policy and the irony, not explained in realist analysis, that multilateralism, including the liberal internationalist regimes and institutions developed after World War II, have offered one of the best guarantees of survival for small states in the post-World War II period. They have done so not just through traditional collective security measures, but by institutionalizing and upholding the norms of non-intervention and non-use-of-force. Theories of international relations which ignore the role of norms and ideas are hardpressed to explain why Singapore as a quintessential realist actor has placed so much faith in global multilateralism.

Even more important is Singapore's role in developing ASEAN as a vehicle for intra-mural conflict avoidance, and to engage through ASEAN in what the founding Foreign Minister, S. Rajaratnam, saw as foreign policy adjustments that would "marry national thinking with regional thinking" and to accept the fact of its "regional existence",[3] precisely the way social constructivism would have put it (i.e., through interaction, states develop a social existence and identity). Throughout the past decades, Singapore has provided new ideas (again a social constructivist mechanism for change and order-building, while realists do not take the role of ideas in international relations seriously) regarding ASEAN cooperation, including AFTA and ASEAN Economic Community. More recently, as

---

[3] Statement by S. Rajaratnam, at the Opening Ceremony of the Inaugural Meeting of the Foreign Ministers of the Association of Southeast Asian Nations, August 8, 1967 (included in the Appendix of this book).

discussed in Chapters 3–5, Singapore has taken a great deal of interest in inter-regionalism. It was the originator of the East Asia–Latin America Dialogue as well as the Asia–Middle East Dialogue. If regionalism, as realists would claim, is but a futile exercise for a region marked by tremendous physical, cultural and political diversity, why would Singapore invest so much of its diplomatic time and energy in it?

A word about Singapore's regional environment is in order here. It is often said, from a realist perspective, that Singapore "suffers its region" and needs to "leapfrog" it in order to achieve security and prosperity. This is misleading, to say the least. Compared to small states in many other parts of the world, such as the Middle East and South Asia, Singapore as a small state enjoys one of the most benign regional environments. Since the end of Sukarno's *Konfrontasi*, Singapore has not faced a predatory neighbor. There is no power of India's or China's intimidating size or Iraq's (under the Saddam Hussein regime) and Iran's geopolitical ambition in Singapore's immediate neighborhood. Instead, ASEAN, for all its limitations, has offered Singapore a largely non-coercive neighborhood within which the city-state can pursue its economic development and ensure its national security. Part of the credit for this must go to Singapore's foreign policymakers, who have maintained its engagement in regional institutions. Singapore's ASEAN neighbors, especially Indonesia, have pursued a remarkably positive attitude towards its independence and territorial integrity. Similarly, geography has been a helpful factor, rather than a constraining one, in Singapore's foreign policy and national security. The perils of limited geographic depth has been more than offset by a locational advantage which the country's leaders have exploited fully to make it a hub of international commerce, which in turn has given the major Western powers and Japan (and now India and China as well) a stake in Singapore's security and well-being. In short, realist narratives of Singapore's foreign policy underplay the extent to which the regional environment has been an asset for Singapore's foreign policy.

Conclusion

Realists often view international cooperation, including participation in international institutions, as a form of "cheap talk" (a game theoretic concept).[4] States may speak the language of cooperation because it makes them look good, but costs little and would have little effect on their actual behavior. It is possible that Singapore's foreign policymakers might have occasionally engaged in such "cheap talk" about regional cooperation. But realism and power balancing can also be a form of "cheap talk", a profoundly legitimizing rhetoric, easier to sell to a domestic audience which expects its leaders to be hardnosed defenders of the national interest, and to Great Power friends who do not want their patronage to be wasted on "starry-eyed" rulers of smaller nations. Hence, small states may actually build interdependence and engage in substantial cooperation while speaking the language of hardnosed *realpolitik*.

The conventional view of Singapore's foreign policy — that it practises an uncompromising approach to regional order in which national defense capabilities and balance of power considerations reign supreme — obscures a more complex picture in which regional interdependence and interactions have held a prominent place. Even when its instincts may be fiercely competitive and zero-sum, cooperation is forced on the city-state by geographic realities and an evolving world order in which "national interest" is deeply enmeshed in regional existence and international interdependence. Contrary to the realist belief that international anarchy (in the sense of having no higher authority above the state) makes competition and rivalry inevitable and cooperation unlikely among states, Singapore's foreign policy experience demonstrates that anarchy can push states towards socialization and cooperation, and even

---

[4] Joseph Farrell and Mathew Rabin, "Cheap Talk", *Journal of Economic Perspectives*, vol. 10, no. 3, 1996, pp. 103–118; Stephen J. Majeski and Shane Fricks, "Conflict and Cooperation in International Relations", *Journal of Conflict Resolution*, vol. 39, no. 4, 1995, pp. 622–645.

collective identity building. In this regard, Singapore's region has not been a "jungle out there", and its search for regional order is not to be understood as a matter of "Singapore suffering the region". "Leapfrogging" or ignoring the region is enormously costly and is not an option for Singapore. It is rather a matter of Singapore's foreign policymakers navigating through the constraints and opportunities offered by its regional environment, which both shapes and is shaped by its foreign policy.

In sum, understanding and explaining Singapore's foreign policy requires us to go beyond the analytic lens offered by realism or the narratives of survival found in most available literature on the subject. While the realist underpinnings of its foreign policy are important and still relevant, they only offer partial accounts of Singapore's foreign policy. This collection of essays, by extending the line of analysis beyond the "narrative of survival" found in most available accounts of Singapore's foreign policy, will help to bring academic analysis closer to the practice of foreign policy in the island-state.

Part I

FOUNDATIONS

1

The Evolution of Singapore's Foreign Policy: Challenges of Change[1]

Introduction

The foreign policy of Singapore, an island- and city-state with an area of 660 square kilometers and population of 3.1 million, is said to be governed by the imperatives of a small state.[2] Dynamism, change and constant adjustment are qualities

[1] Paper presented to the Conference on "The Political Economy of Foreign Policy in Southeast Asia", University of Windsor, Windsor, Ontario, October 29–November 1, 1992. The author would like to acknowledge helpful discussions on the theme of the paper with Mr S. Rajaratnam, Singapore's first Foreign Minister and a former Deputy Prime Minister; Mr Peter Chan Jer Hing, Permanent Secretary in the Ministry of Foreign Affairs, Singapore; Professor Chan Heng Chee, Director of Singapore International Foundation; and Dr N. Ganesan of the Department of Political Science, National University of Singapore.

[2] Obaid ul Haq, "Foreign Policy", in Jon S.T. Quah, Chan Heng Chee and Seah Chee Meow, eds., *Government and Politics of Singapore*, Singapore, Oxford University Press, 1987, pp. 276–308; Bilveer Singh, *Singapore: Foreign Policy Imperatives of a Small State*, National University of Singapore, Centre for Advanced Studies, 1988; and Chan Heng Chee, "Singapore: Domestic Structure and Foreign Policy", in Robert Scalapino, Jusuf Wanandi and Sung-Joo Han, eds., *Regional Dynamics: Security, Political and Economic Issues in the Asia-Pacific Region*, Jakarta, Centre for Strategic and International Studies, 1990; Linda Lim, "Singapore's Foreign Policy", in David Wurfel and Bruce Burton, eds., *The Political Economy of Foreign Policy in Southeast Asia*, London, Macmillan, 1990; and M. Ramesh, "Economic Globalization and Policy Choices: Singapore", *Governance*, vol. 8, no. 2, 1995, pp. 243–260.

usually associated with the foreign policy behavior of small states. The contemporary international system has gone through a major upheaval as the result of events associated largely, but not exclusively, with the end of the Cold War. These changes have altered the political, strategic and economic context of foreign policy-making for states, both at the systemic and regional levels. Singapore is no exception. But what exactly has been Singapore's response to the challenges of change?

This paper attempts to address this question in four parts. The first looks at the basic and enduring features of Singapore's foreign policy and the impact of the Cold War in shaping them. This is followed by an examination of national power elements as well as the foreign policy decision-making apparatus that have helped Singapore manage its vulnerabilities. The third part analyzes the challenges that Singapore's foreign policy-makers face in adjusting to post-Cold War realities. The fourth part examines foreign policy output, i.e., Singapore's responses to the issues arising in the post-Cold War environment.

Realism and Survival

Singapore's foreign policy-makers have articulated an essentially realist conception of international politics. As former Foreign Minister S. Dhanabalan argued:

> The international system comprises sovereign states each admitting to no authority except its own. International relations therefore resembles a Hobbesian state of nature, where each is pitted against all. In such a potentially anarchic situation, order is the prime value. In international politics, as in national politics, order is prior to justice, to morality, to economic prosperity, to any other value that you can think of simply because, in the absence of order, no other value can be realised. In the absence of order the life of states would be as in the life of men in the state of nature — "Nasty, Brutish and Short."[3]

---

[3] S. Dhanabalan, Text of a talk at the National University of Singapore Forum, November 27, 1981 (included in the Appendix of this book).

In more recent times, this severe *realpolitik* view has been moderated somewhat. There is greater recognition of the impact of interdependence in constraining the use of force in international relations. The role of regional and global institutions in promoting cooperation is viewed as constituting an important basis for foreign policy action. This is not to say that Singapore's leaders have converted to a more idealistic conception of international politics. The essence of twentieth-century Idealism, the doctrine of collective security, does not enjoy much credibility in the minds of Singapore's leaders in relation to the realist conception of balance of power.

In an anarchic international system, survival and security are the highest goals for states. For a small state like Singapore, ensuring survival, both in a physical and economic sense, has been especially crucial.[4] The emphasis on survival in foreign policy reflects major vulnerabilities of the city-state in the domestic and external arena. Singapore's predicament as a country without any natural resources and a small domestic market creates inherent obstacles to economic development. Similarly, a multiethnic social fabric makes the task of ensuring national integration, and hence national security, a difficult challenge. In addition, managing domestic political order and continuity has also been an important aspect of vulnerability and survival. As Chan Heng Chee writes, "survival" was "a political theme adopted by the PAP leaders to justify their domestic and international policies and to mobilise the island population to greater efforts".[5] In this sense, pursuit of survival in foreign policy would contribute not only to the security of the state, but also to the security of the regime as well. In Rajaratnam's own words: "our approach has always been to shape the kind of foreign policy that will consolidate our domestic position, resolve some of our domestic problems and enhance our security, and our economic and political strength".[6]

---

[4] N. Ganesan, "Singapore's Foreign Policy Terrain", *Asian Affairs: An American Review*, vol. 19, no. 2, 1992, pp. 67–79; Leszek Buszynski, "Singapore: A Foreign Policy of Survival", *Asian Thought and Society*, July 29, 1985, pp. 128–136.

[5] Chan Heng Chee, *Singapore: The Politics of Survival: 1965–1967*, Singapore, Oxford University Press, 1971, p. 1.

[6] Rajaratnam, cited in Singh, *Singapore: Foreign Policy Imperatives of a Small State*, p. 12.

In the external sphere, Singapore's vulnerability is rooted in both geostrategic and historical factors. Singapore's location as a small Chinese-majority state in close proximity to large Malay neighbors contributes to a deep-rooted insecurity *vis-à-vis* the two immediately adjacent neighbors. This insecurity was compounded by the circumstances of Singapore's separation from the Malaysian federation in 1965 and the hostility shown towards Singapore by Indonesia during and in the immediate aftermath of "Konfrontasi".[7] As a historical event, Konfrontasi remains entrenched in the minds of Singapore's leadership as an example of what might happen if regional neighbors are to be ruled by nationalistic regimes. In general, vulnerability remains a key theme of Singapore's foreign policy; as recently as in 1988, Foreign Minister Wong Kan Seng issued a reminder that:

> The vulnerability of small states is a fact of life. Singapore's independent existence is today widely recognised. But to assure our basic security, we can never allow tests to our sovereignty and internal affairs, even when well-intentioned, to go unchallenged. Even today, we have had occasionally to remind other countries to leave us alone to be ourselves.[8]

The Cold War superpower rivalry aggravated Singapore's vulnerabilities as a small state. But "Realism in international politics consists not only of acknowledging limits, but also recognizing opportunities".[9] Thus, Singapore not only recognized, but also deftly exploited, opportunities in both the geopolitical as well as economic arena created by the Cold War. Geopolitically, the Cold War was marked by a regional balance of power which favored Singapore's survival and well-being. As Singapore saw it, "a multiplicity of external Great Powers involved in the region, balancing each other" would not only ensure regional stability, but "allow small states to survive in the interstices between them". Such a situation

---

[7] Michael Leifer, *Indonesian Foreign Policy*, London, George Allen & Unwin, 1983, p. 123.

[8] Wong Kan Seng, "Continuity and Change in Singapore's Foreign Policy", Speech to the Singapore Press Club, November 15, 1988.

[9] Dhanabalan, *op. cit.*

would be preferable to "less manageable small power rivalries".[10] The Cold War in Asia also contributed to Singapore's economic prosperity. Singapore's success in securing a steady flow of foreign investments and access to Western markets was helped by the Republic's essentially anti-communist and pro-Western foreign policy outlook. By fashioning itself as a "global city" — i.e., by rapidly integrating itself into the international market economy and according a very hospitable welcome to Western multinationals at a time when much of the Third World was suspicious of them — Singapore was able to create a stake of the West in its survival and prosperity.[11]

In general, the Cold War and bipolar international system was a period of relative stability for Singapore. Superpower rivalry, despite its role in fueling regional conflict, was marked by some "rules of the game". A certain degree of predictability in Great Power action provided small states with opportunities to enhance the conditions of their survival.

National Capacity and Foreign Policy Decision-Making

As the foregoing discussion suggests, survival, national security and economic well-being would rank among the major objectives of Singapore foreign policy. In pursuing these goals, Singapore's foreign policy-makers have been helped by a number of factors, of which four are especially noteworthy: economic capacity, military strength, bureaucratic apparatus and the nature of the political system as it affects foreign policy formulation.

Singapore's economic success is well-known and documented. Singapore today ranks as the world's 18th richest nation, with a per capita GDP of US$13,500 in 1991. Economic success, to the extent that it owes to development of global trade and investment linkages,

---

[10] Dhanabalan, cited in Singh, *Singapore: Foreign Policy Imperatives of a Small State*, pp. 32–33.
[11] See Chapter 2 of this book.

also shapes foreign policy capabilities and goals. In 1991, Singapore's total trade amounted to $216 billion. Singapore was the world's seventh largest exporter and fifteenth largest importer. Singapore is also the world's most trade-dependent nation, and has the highest trade to GDP ratio, trade being 3 times the GDP. Thus, economic issues including development of new trade opportunities and preservation of market access have an unusual salience among foreign policy objectives. In addition, Singapore's economic power and potential also enables it, at least in theory, to pursue foreign policy goals quite out of proportion to its physical size or population.

Secondly, economic success has contributed to the development of a powerful military deterrent. In 1992, the Singapore Armed Forces (SAF) consisted of some 50,000 regulars and 250,000 reservists. Combining the best features of Swiss-style citizen's army and Israeli-style forward defense, Singapore's Armed Forces complement foreign policy not only by securing its basic objectives of national security and survival, but also in providing the basis of a more assured and confident position on vital international issues. Although "military defense" is only one of the five aspects of Singapore's "Total Defense" policy (the others being psychological, social, civil and economic defense), the military sector absorbs considerable resources. Singapore's defense spending is pegged at 6 percent of its GDP, which in FY1992 amounted to $4 billion.[12] A recent Asian Development Bank report has put Singapore as the leading country in Asia in defense spending measured in per capita terms as well as percentage of total government spending.[13] Not surprisingly, Singapore can afford to field the most modern military hardware in Southeast Asia.

Third, Singapore's foreign policy capacity also rests on a growing and sophisticated bureaucratic apparatus dedicated to ensuring the country's "security, prosperity and international standing and

---

[12] Ministry of Defense, Singapore, 1992, p. 46.
[13] *Far Eastern Economic Review*, April 30, 1992, p. 53.

influence".[14] Singapore's Foreign Ministry was established in August 1965 and an exclusive Foreign Service was constituted in 1972. The number of foreign missions has increased from only five in 1966 to 26 in 1992. Changes in the organizational structure of the foreign ministry are also indicative of new policy directions to deal with developments in the regional and international arena. The growing importance of the Asia-Pacific region is reflected in the creation of a new directorate covering East Asia, Australia and New Zealand. A technical training directorate has been set up to facilitate collaboration with developing countries and international organizations. Moreover, between 1989 and 1992, three new missions were opened, all of them being in the Asia-Pacific region: Korea (1989), Beijing (1990) and Hanoi (1992).

Fourth, Singapore's foreign policy decision-making process remains unencumbered by any domestic political constraints.[15] The opposition parties have not been critical of the government's handling of foreign affairs. The parliamentary consultative process on foreign affairs and defense was somewhat downgraded after the 1991 general elections in an apparent bid by the government to shore up PAP unity and central control. Foreign policy decisions in Singapore are usually made at the highest level. The former Prime Minister of Singapore, Mr Lee Kuan Yew, remains an articulate spokesman of Singapore's international concerns and policies as a sort of elder statesman and "official mascot" of the Republic.

Neither is Singapore's foreign policy responsive to domestic pressure groups, simply because such groups do not exist. Nor, unlike many developing countries, has the Singapore government felt the need to mobilize its population in support of specific foreign policy goals. It has been concerned, however, that foreign policy decisions do not endanger domestic stability. This is especially true of foreign policy decisions that have a bearing on ethnic relations, with a major example being the government's position that Singapore's

---

[14] Ministry of Foreign Affairs, Singapore, 1992, p. 1.

[15] ul Haq, *op. cit.*

diplomatic relations with China should await normalization of Sino-Indonesian ties.

Viewed in terms of its basic objectives, Singapore's foreign policy has been remarkably successful. Not only has Singapore preserved its sovereign statehood, but it has also achieved spectacular economic success and firmly established the means of defending its prosperity. Thus, Singapore's foreign policy managers should be well-placed to face the changes ushered by the end of the Cold War. But the fact that no such complacency is evident in their thinking owes to a belief that the end of the Cold War has given way to a much more complex and fluid regional and international environment within which foreign policy must be framed. This has given rise to a number of specific concerns which must be addressed to ensure the realization of foreign policy goals in the post-Cold War era.

The Changing Context

While the end of the Cold War generated a great deal of optimism about the future of the international system, none was more so than the vision of a "New World Order" outlined by the Bush administration in the wake of the Iraqi invasion of Kuwait in August 1990. Although the term remains extremely vague and ill-defined, one could discern at least two senses in which it has been used. First, in its normative sense, the New World Order represents an ideal, a vision of international relations cherished by those who reject ideological polarization, power politics and geopolitical competition within the international system. In addition, New World Order involves a call for greater equality and justice in the conduct of international relations and the replacement of balance of power geopolitics with a system of collective security. But the term "New World Order" is also used in a second, and somewhat descriptive sense, to simply refer to the momentous developments of the past few years culminating in the demise of the bipolar international order. These changes, such the collapse of communism in Europe, the fall of the Berlin Wall, the break-up of the Soviet Union, the spread of democracy in Europe and the Third World, do not necessarily imply any idealistic aspirations for a better world, but simply an awareness that states and leaders must now relate to a new international milieu in the conduct of their foreign relations.

In so far as Singapore is concerned, the slogan of the New World Order in its idealistic sense is clearly at variance with the realities of international life. As Chan Heng Chee writes, "even before Iraq's invasion of Kuwait, Singapore espoused the worldview that the end of the Cold War need not lead to an epidemic of peace".[16] But even as they expressed doubts about the New World Order as an ideal, Singapore's leaders were swift to recognize the dimensions of a New World Order in its descriptive sense. Senior Minister Lee Kuan Yew, in his increasingly visible role as an elder statesman, particularly stressed the transition from bipolarity to multipolarity in the international system as a development of immense importance.[17]

In the Third World, the end of the Cold War facilitated the settlement of a number of regional conflicts, the most important development from Singapore's perspective being the withdrawal of Vietnamese forces from Cambodia and the signing of the Paris Peace Agreement in October 1991. Singapore's role in ensuring the international isolation of Vietnam for its invasion of Cambodia had been the high point of its diplomacy. Although the final outcome was orchestrated by the Great Powers involved in the conflict, Singapore hailed the Paris Agreement as "one of the happier outcomes of the new world order that was wrought by the profound and dramatic changes of the last few years".[18] Arguably, during the final stages of the Cambodia peace process, Singapore, identified with the so-called "hardline camp" within ASEAN, was somewhat distressed by Thailand's move to improve ties with the Phnom Penh

---

[16] Chan Heng Chee, "Singapore 1991: Dealing with a Post-Cold War World", in Lee Tsao Yuan, ed., *Singapore: The Year in Review*, Singapore, Times Academic Press for Institute of Policy Studies, 1992.

[17] Lee Kuan Yew, Text of speech at a banquet hosted by the Lord Mayor of London, May 24, 1990.

[18] Wong Kan Seng, Statement at the Paris Conference on Cambodia, October 23, 1991.

regime and the US decision to withdraw recognition from the
Coalition Government of Democratic Kampuchea (CDGK) which
included the genocidal Khmer Rouge. In general, however, the
Cambodia agreement augured well for Singapore's strategic and
economic interests in the Asia-Pacific region as it marked the end of
the "larger conflicts that characterized the international system for
much of the post-Cold War period".[19]

But Singapore is not unduely optimistic about the regional political environment. Its leaders perceive the danger of new regional
conflicts, e.g., the Spratly Islands, Korean Peninsula, and Singapore's
own dispute with Malaysia over the Pedra Branca island off the coast
of Johor.

For Singapore, these conflicts would not matter if the regional
balance of power underpinned by forward deployed US military
forces remained intact. But this cannot be assured. The withdrawal
of US bases from the Philippines has been the single most important
concern, although Singapore is also worried about the future of US
military presence in Japan and Korea and the uncertainties facing
the US-Japan security alliance. A related threat to the regional balance of power is the prospect of a more assertive role by regional
powers such as China, Japan and India in the post-Cold War milieu.

Such apprehensions are matched by a concern that the global
geopolitical divide of the past might be replaced by economic conflicts. As Lee Kuan Yew put it, "In future, competition between
industrialized nations will be primarily economic, and this competition will be worldwide".[20] Moreover, such competition might also
undermine international regimes such as the General Agreement
on Tariffs and Trade (GATT) and encourage exclusionary regional
trading blocs.[21] The latter would threaten Singapore's prosperity
by diverting trade and investment away from the Southeast Asian
region.

---

[19] *Ibid.*

[20] Lee Kuan Yew, *op. cit.*

[21] Goh Chok Tong, Address before the Eighth Pacific Economic Cooperation
Conference, Singapore, May 20–22, 1991.

Moving Beyond Survival

Despite these concerns, one of the most important changes in Singapore's foreign policy is its evolution into a "post-survival" phase. To be sure, some of the survival concerns which were so starkly associated with the management of its most sensitive bilateral relationships, namely with Malaysia and Indonesia, have persisted. Periodic crises in relations with Malaysia (such as the suspension of joint military exercises between the two countries over an alleged spying incident in 1989, Malaysia's protests over Singapore's offer of military facilities to the US and Singapore's protest over the holding of joint exercises between Malaysia and Indonesia in 1991) are a reminder of these concerns, reflecting historical suspicions as well as lingering racial and religious sensitivities that govern the relationship between the two countries.[22] But there has also been the emergence of a structure of stability that combines a pragmatic approach to crisis management on the part of the top leaders (of both countries) with an effort to develop longer-term functional linkages (such as ASEAN, the Growth Triangle, the Five Power Defense Arrangements), which lessen the incentive to resort to force. It remains to be seen, however, whether this structure of stability can survive the process of regime/leadership change that confronts Indonesia and Malaysia. But Singapore has come a long way from its post-independence vulnerabilities as "a Chinese island in a sea of Malays".

Survival concerns are also still reflected in Singapore's desire to ensure a favorable balance of power in the Asia-Pacific region. Singapore sees no credible alternative security arrangement in the Asia-Pacific region that can be "as comfortable as the present one

---

[22] N. Ganesan, "Factors Affecting Singapore's Foreign Policy towards Malaysia", *Australian Journal of International Affairs*, vol. 45, no. 2, 1991, pp. 182–195. See also, R.S. Milner, "Singapore's Exit from Malaysia: The Consequences of Ambiguity", *Asian Survey*, vol. 9, no. 3, March 1966, pp. 175–184; Lau Teik Soon, "Malaysia-Singapore Relations: Crisis of Adjustment, 1965–68", *Journal of Southeast Asian History*, vol. 10, March 1969, pp. 155–176.

with the US as the major player".[23] Proposals for a multilateral security mechanism, as suggested by Australia, Canada and Russia, are not seen to be adequate in this regard and might undermine the relevance of existing US alliances which must be maintained in order to offset the possibility of Indonesia's assertiveness, Japanese remilitarization, and deter possible Chinese ambitions in the South China Sea area.

Singapore's role in preserving the regional balance of power has been to provide military facilities to the US. A Memorandum of Understanding signed in November 1990 provided for the deployment of US military personnel in Singapore and the rotating deployment of US fighter aircrafts. During President Bush's visit to Singapore on January 3–5, 1992, the two countries reached an agreement on the relocation of a naval logistics facility from Subic Bay. Singapore also continues to support the Five Power Defense Arrangements (FPDA), involving itself, Malaysia, Australia, New Zealand and the United Kingdom. Although the FPDA is widely seen as an alliance without real teeth, Singapore believes that it is useful as a deterrent as well as a bridge between Singapore and Malaysia, and as a model for other forms of multilateral defense cooperation among ASEAN states.

The evolution of regionalism in Southeast Asia has been a key anchor of Singapore's foreign policy success and it is to this arena that the government has devoted a great deal of its diplomatic attention in the post-Cold War era. Singapore's leaders recognize ASEAN's contribution in stabilizing its regional security environment. But with the end of the Cambodian conflict, Foreign Minister Wong Kan Seng expressed concern that ASEAN's future "cannot be taken for granted" and that ASEAN would require "new rallying points or risk drifting apart to the detriment of regional cooperation and bilateral relationships".[24]

---

[23] *The Straits Times*, October 2, 1992, p. 13.

[24] Wong Kan Seng, Text of speech at Defence Asia '89 Conference on "Towards Greater ASEAN Military Cooperation: Issues and Prospects", Singapore, March 24, 1989.

Singapore contributed to ending the uncertainty about ASEAN's future by hosting the fourth ASEAN summit in January 1992. The summit and subsequent ASEAN-sponsored meetings (including the July 1993 ASEAN Foreign Ministers' meeting held in Singapore) have paved the way for ASEAN to assume a formal role in regional security issues. Although ASEAN would not be turned into a military alliance, it would hold multilateral consultations over security issues within the framework of a newly-established ASEAN Regional Forum.[25] In the economic arena, ASEAN has adopted the goal of an ASEAN Free Trade Area (AFTA) to take effect from the year 2003.

The emphasis on economic regionalism is an important development. Singapore's economic prosperity is based on its strategy of "globalization". But in recent years, its leaders have seen economic regionalization as a necessary, indeed inevitable, response to the crisis in the global economy.[26] In the past twenty years, Singapore's trade has moved away from the Southeast Asian region, so that trade with ASEAN has been overtaken by trade with the US, Japan and the European Community. Similarly, most of the foreign investment in Singapore comes from the US, Japan and Europe. But the current crisis in GATT, the emergence of regional trade arrangements in Europe and North America, the trend towards market-oriented reforms in Southeast Asia and the dramatic growth in trade and investment linkages between East Asia and Southeast Asia have led Singapore to look more closely at regional trade and investment opportunities. This involves not only developing new markets in the region, but encouraging Singaporean investments in southern China, Vietnam and ASEAN. Singapore's conception of regional cooperation is broad and flexible — "regional" in the economic sense consists of three layers: ASEAN; a subregional layer consisting of Singapore, Malaysia and Indonesia; and a macro-regional layer encompassing Eastern Asia and Asia-Pacific.

At the subregional level, Singapore has advocated the concept of "market-driven regionalism". This is in part a recognition of the

---

[25] See Chapter 2 of this book.

[26] *Ibid.*

limitations of government-led approach to ASEAN economic integration, which has thus far produced only limited results. Singapore's initiative on the "Growth Triangle", incorporating Singapore, Batam (about two-thirds of the size of Singapore) and the Riau Islands of Indonesia and Johor in Malaysia, is illustrative of the new approach. The Growth Triangle is supposed to combine Singapore's financial services with abundant cheap labor and land in Johor and Batam, and thereby benefit all parties by offsetting Singapore's scarcity of land and manpower and attracting foreign investors to Johor and Batam.

Apart from the Growth Triangle concept (which has been greeted somewhat coolly by the Malaysian federal government), the creation of the ASEAN Free Trade Area assumes importance as the second tier of regional economic cooperation for Singapore. To realize the AFTA concept in 15 years, ASEAN envisages a progressive lowering and harmonization of tariffs within the grouping to an eventual rate of between 0.5%–5%. It should be noted, however, that AFTA's scope as a trade-liberalization measure also faces a number of barriers, including questions over the speed of sectoral liberalization and concerns over unequal distribution of benefits. Some members, like Thailand, face complaints from their manufacturers that a speedy implementation of AFTA might see their uncompetitive products being swamped by cheaper and better quality imports from more advanced ASEAN countries, while others, like Indonesia, fear a huge loss of revenues for government expenditure arising from tariff cuts envisaged by AFTA.

Thus, a mere deepening of ASEAN economic cooperation through AFTA is not enough to counter the economic problems of the 1990s. Wider regional economic forums in the Asia-Pacific region are also important in this respect. In recent years, two such frameworks have emerged. The first is Asia-Pacific Economic Cooperation forum (APEC), a loose forum of Asia-Pacific nations which disavows protectionism and promotes cooperation. The second is a proposal made by Prime Minister Mahathir Mohammed of Malaysia in December 1990 for an East Asia Economic Grouping (later changed to East Asian Economic Caucus) to "counter the threat of protectionism and regionalism in world trade".

ASEAN's attitude towards APEC was initially colored by a fear that the latter might detract from the former's own role in promoting regional cooperation. But Singapore viewed ASEAN and APEC as "really concentric circles",[27] and that APEC could be useful in multilateral trade negotiations.[28] The successful bid to host the APEC secretariat in Singapore demonstrated Singapore's interest in the institution. In contrast, the EAEC concept has received only qualified support. During a visit to Malaysia in January 1991, Prime Minister Goh appeared to recognize the potential of EAEC to "boost the multilateral free trade system, supplement ASEAN economic cooperation, and give greater meaning to APEC". But he hastened to add that efforts to pursue the proposed framework should be undertaken "without jeopardizing our traditionally important trading ties".[29] This is bound to be difficult in view of the strong US opposition to the idea and the related lack of enthusiasm on the part of Japan to endorse the concept. In July 1993, Singapore helped to devise a compromise formula which would make EAEC a consultative mechanism within APEC, rather than an independent institution, although EAEC's future remains constrained by differences and tensions between Malaysia and the US (as well as Australia).

As the preceding discussion shows, Singapore's post-Cold War foreign policy is dominated by the twin themes of regionalization in the economic arena and a regional balance of power in the political-security arena. These two factors also shape Singapore's evolving relationship with China, which has experienced something of a revolution in recent years. Singapore's leaders, particularly Lee Kuan Yew, see China as the most significant player affecting the balance of power in the Asia-Pacific region. China also offers immense

---

[27] *Far Eastern Economic Review*, November 16, 1989.

[28] Lee Hsien Loong, Speech before the Indonesia Forum, Jakarta, July 11, 1990.

[29] *The Business Times*, January 12–13, 1991.

opportunities to develop an "external wing" of Singapore's heavily foreign trade- and investment-dependent economy. Since formal diplomatic relations were established in 1990 (in keeping with Singapore's stated policy of being the last ASEAN country to do so, in deference to the anti-Chinese sentiments of its Malay neighbors), trade and investment links between the two countries have risen sharply, helped by considerable government encouragement and support which includes a call to Singaporean Chinese investors to take advantage of traditional ethnic ties with China. Bilateral trade between the countries was valued at S\$5.5 billion in 1992, while Singapore has emerged as one of the largest foreign investors in China with some 1,300 projects and a total contracted investment figure of \$1.8 billion in 1992.[30] Frequent visits by senior Singapore leaders underscore the growing salience of China in Singapore's foreign policy. Lee Kuan Yew has often spoken out in favor of China's international concerns, and opposed US economic sanctions against China on the basis of its poor human rights record. Singapore has strongly and successfully argued for the inclusion of China in ASEAN's framework for multilateral security consultations on security issues in the Asia-Pacific region. To be sure, a special relationship between Singapore and China remains constrained by Singapore's deference to sensitivities in Malaysia and Indonesia (where the rapid growth of Sino-Singapore ties is not entirely welcome), not to mention within Singapore's own non-Chinese population. Nonetheless, the rapid proliferation of economic and political links with China reflect the lessening of its survival concerns.

A final aspect of Singapore's foreign policy also attests to the growing importance of post-survival issues. This relates to a somewhat paradoxical impact of the New World Order on Singapore's foreign policy concerns. On the one hand, the "New World Order" is associated with a reinvigorated UN role in international peace and security, a development which has presented Singapore with opportunities to play a more active role in UN peacekeeping and

---

[30] *Ibid.*; *The Straits Times*, May 7, 1993.

enforcement operations. Since 1990, Singapore has participated in several such operations: Cambodia (1992–1993), Namibia (1990), Western Sahara (1991), Angola (1991), Saudi Arabia (1991) and the Iraq-Kuwait border (1991). The impression of foreign policy activism has also been fueled by the establishment of the Singapore International Foundation (SIF) in August 1991, with its stated goal of helping the Republic to "play a more dynamic and mature role in the international arena" and thereby "make a contribution to the world at large". Although a major aim of the SIF is to maintain contacts with Singaporeans abroad, it is also responsible for the creation of a Singaporean "peace corps" to provide humanitarian service in poorer countries. Post-survival foreign policy activism is also evident in Singapore's growing ability to provide technical assistance (mainly human resource development) to other developing countries which (including China) have expressed an interest in learning from Singapore's successful development experience. During the past decade, some 21,500 foreign participants from over 87 countries have received technical training in Singapore under various schemes and arrangements with the United Nations and other international organizations (such as ASEAN and Colombo Plan). Singapore has also initiated programs jointly with other countries such as Japan to provide technical training for developing countries in Asia and Africa.

On the other hand, the end of the East-West ideological struggle has propeled certain North-South political issues such as human rights, environment and democratization into the international limelight. Indeed, these issues are viewed by Singapore officials as major challenges for the ASEAN states in the post-Cold War era. Singapore's position on human rights and democratization consists of a number of elements: rejection of Western claims about the universality of human rights; opposition to any attempt by the Western countries to "impose any particular political pattern or special arrangement" to promote human rights; rejection of any linkage of foreign aid to human rights performance; highlighting of the selective, even inconsistent, promotion of human rights by the Western countries; and emphasizing the greater importance of economic

growth, order and stability in relation to human rights and democratization.[31] While these positions parallel those of many other
developing countries, Singapore's leaders are sensitive to being
labeled as part of the "hardliner" camp on these issues among the
developing countries. They are also cognizant of the danger that the
emerging North-South divisions on human rights could transform
the vision of a "New World Order" into a "New Cold War", which
must be avoided through compromise and consensus. It should be
noted, however, that Singapore, which is less vulnerable to Western
human rights pressure due to its lack of need for foreign development assistance and which does not face a domestic insurgency
attracting the attention of Western human rights groups, can afford
to be more "moderate" than other developing countries on the issue
of human rights and democratization. But there is no question that
Singapore's foreign policy concerns are increasingly sensitive to the
growing politicization of these issues which could undermine its
international image (and interest) even if they do not threaten the
country's physical or economic well-being.

Conclusion

Although Singapore's foreign policy-makers recognize the impact of
profound and far-reaching changes to the international system
resulting from the end of superpower rivalry, the prospect for a fundamental transformation of the power politics paradigm is viewed by
them with a great deal of skepticism. The end of the Cold War is no
reason for complacency, and the slogan for a "New World Order",
especially in its normative/idealistic aspects, is too vague to constitute the proper basis for foreign policy action.

    Nonetheless, Singapore's severe *realpolitik* view of international
relations has been moderated by a recognition of the opportunities
for multilateral cooperation and institution-building. Some of these
opportunities predated the end of the Cold War, but some are also

---

[31] *The Straits Times*, June 17, 1993.

a direct result of the reduction in global and regional tensions in the Cold War's wake. Accordingly, Singapore's foreign policy output has moved on two parallel tracks. On the one hand, Singapore has been quite active in expanding existing and potential avenues of multilateral cooperation in political and economic spheres. On the other hand, new security challenges in the region and lingering regional suspicions and rivalries have ensured continued faith in externally-linked security arrangements that promote a balance of power in the region. In short, Singapore's foreign policy in the post-Cold War era is geared to promoting institutionalization in the regional political economy, while preserving existing security arrangements that date back to the Cold War period.

At the same time, Singapore's foreign policy has gradually accommodated more internationalist concerns, reflecting its economic success and greater political confidence. The Cambodia conflict was the turning point in Singapore's diplomacy, but more recently, initiatives undertaken in the area of international peacekeeping and technical assistance to developing countries clearly imply a more dynamic foreign policy commensurate with the growing international recognition of its economic success.

Nonetheless, Singapore's foreign policy continues to be geared essentially to overcoming vulnerabilities, both old and new. While Singapore's traditional vulnerabilities such as smallness and location have been successfully managed, thanks to a thriving economy, stable polity and growing military strength, its extraordinary dependence on foreign trade and external security guarantees creates new sources of vulnerability. In this context, the Cold War and related changes in the global economy have raised serious challenges. The Cold War, despite the dangers it posed to the security of small states, was nonetheless a relatively manageable framework of international relations for Singapore. It imparted a greater degree of predictability to the system of Great Power relations and ensured a bipolar balance of power in the international system, whose regional dynamics were generally in Singapore's interest. The post-Cold War setting is much more fluid, and contains important risks such as that of economic competition, regional conflicts and uncertainties of balance of power. The very unpredictability of post-Cold War geopolitics induces caution and a certain amount of anxiety. Of particular significance are the economic challenges arising out of the crisis in the international trade regime, but strategic retrenchments by Great Powers and shifting balance of power in the Asia-Pacific region have also been perceived to be crucial challenges to Singapore's foreign policy-makers. To manage these challenges is the foremost task of Singapore's foreign policy. By making full use of the experience of the past decades and the increased capabilities and resources on hand, Singapore's foreign policy-makers are confident of meeting this challenge. As they see it, the end of the Cold War may not necessarily mean that the international environment has become friendlier to small states, but only that successful small states like Singapore have become more adept at operating at the international level to ensure their interests and objectives.

2

The Economic Foundations of Singapore's Security: From Globalism to Regionalism?[1]

Co-authored with M. Ramesh

I t is well-recognized that Singapore's economic success is built on the global economy. What is not recognized is that the global economy is the foundation of its national security as well. This chapter will elaborate upon the latter point. It will then examine changes in the global economic environment which have necessitated greater emphasis on regional economic cooperation. The purpose of the inquiry is to examine the global economy's contribution to Singapore's national security and assess the extent to which it is possible for the city-state to depend on the regional economy for its national security.

National security is a complex and controversial concept. In the traditional realist literature, national security is defined as protection of the state's "core values" — political sovereignty and territorial integrity — from external military threats.[2] In this view, national

---

[1] This paper, co-written with M. Ramesh, was discussed at a seminar entitled "ASEAN Round Table: ASEAN Economic Co-operation in the 1980s", jointly held by the Institute of Southeast Asian Studies and the Institute of Policy Studies in Singapore, June 27–28, 1991. It was subsequently published as a chapter in Garry Rodan, ed., *Singapore Changes Guard: Social, Political and Economic Directions in the 1990s*, Sydney, Longman Cheshire, 1993, pp. 134–152.

[2] Walter Lippmann, *US Foreign Policy: The Sword of the Republic*, Boston, Little, Brown, 1943, p. 150.

security is seen as lying primarily in a state's own military strength and its military alliances with other states. Recent literature on the subject, however, challenges the realist emphasis on military force for being too narrow,[3] arguing for a broader interpretation of national security by incorporating non-military, especially economic, threats and vulnerabilities.[4] While it is difficult to rigorously specify the economic foundations of national security, recent works have pointed to two crucial dimensions.

The first concerns the use of economic instruments by the state to overcome its geopolitical vulnerability to external threats. In this sense, the economic elements of national security involve "the ability of a nation to pursue its national interests [including its core values]... using national economic policies if appropriate".[5] A state may employ economic means to achieve external security in two ways. Weak and vulnerable states, unable to assure their self-protection, may offer economic incentives to outside powers in return for their security guarantees. A good example is Saudi Arabia's strategic relationship with the USA, which has acted as the chief security guarantor of the Saudi regime in exchange for assured access to Saudi oil

---

[3] Mohammed Ayoob, ed., *Regional Security in the Third World: Case Studies from Southeast Asia and the Middle East*, London, Croom Helm, 1986, pp. 3–23; Edward E. Azar and Chung-in Moon, eds., *National Security in the Third World: The Management of Internal and External Threats*, Sydney, Edward Elgar, Aldershot, Allen & Unwin, 1988, pp. 1–13; Barry Buzan, *People, States and Fear*, 2nd ed., London, Harvester Wheatsheaf, 1991, pp. 14–43.

[4] Buzan, *ibid.*; Klaus Knorr, *The Power of Nations: The Political Economy of International Relations*, New York, Basic Books, 1975; Stephen D. Krasner, "National Security and Economics", in B. Thomas Trout and James E. Harf, eds., *National Security Affairs, Theoretical Perspectives and Contemporary Issues*, New Brunswick, NJ, Transaction Books, 1982, pp. 313–328; Ethan B. Kapstein, "Economic Development and National Security", in Azar and Moon, *National Security in the Third World*, pp. 136–151; G. Luciani, "The Economic Content of Security", *Journal of Public Policy*, vol. 8, no. 2, 1988, pp. 151–174; Penelope Hartland-Thunberg, "National Economic Security: Interdependence and Vulnerability", in Frans A. M. Alting von Geusau and Jacques Pelkmans, eds., *National Economic Security: Perceptions, Threats and Policies*, The Netherlands, John F. Kennedy Institute, Tilburg, 1982.

[5] Hartland-Thunberg, *ibid.*, p. 51.

supplies. If no such indigenous resources are available to satisfy the needs of the outside power, as is likely in the case of small states, then offering incentives of trade and investment may enable such states to create foreign powers' stakes in their national economies and thereby in their security and survival. The post-war search for foreign production bases by multinational companies (MNCs) offered opportunities for many states to attract both MNCs' investments and the security umbrella of their parent states. Another way for states to achieve external security through economic instruments is to use them as sanctions, either negatively (to punish) or positively (to induce cooperative behavior), in dealing with their adversaries. Small states, lacking the power to coerce adversaries, usually must turn to positive sanctions. A good example of this is Kuwait in the 1970s and 1980s, which used its substantial oil revenues to "buy moderation" on the part of its radical Arab neighbors. In the case of Singapore, economic policies have been geared both to secure protection from friendly external powers as well as to induce moderation on the part of neighbors with whom it has sensitive security relations.

The second linkage between economics and national security has to do with domestic threats to political stability and survival of regimes. These are important, especially in developing countries where national security concerns frequently mask the regime's instinct for self-preservation.[6] While many Third World regimes survive by repression, some survive through legitimacy gained from superior economic performance. Economic prosperity makes regimes less vulnerable to domestic unrest and more resilient to external pressures.[7] Regimes' ability to seek legitimation through economic performance is subject to many constraints. However, small states, which are specially constrained because of their lack of natural resources and the small size of their domestic markets, may offset their limitations by turning to the global economy for economic performance. In such cases, regime legitimation through

---

[6] Ayoob, *op. cit.*

[7] Muthiah Alagappa, *The National Security of a Developing State: Lessons from Thailand*, Dover, Massachusetts, Auburn House, 1987, p. 25.

profitable linkages with the global economy becomes a key component of national security strategy.

"Globalization" in this chapter will be understood as referring to the extent of participation in the global economy. Given the nature of the post-war international economic order, however, global economy for practical purposes means the US-led Western economy. For Singapore, therefore, participation in the global economy has meant developing trade and investment links with the Western countries. "Regionalization" will be understood as referring to developing trade and investment links with the economies within the region. In the case of Singapore, regionalization has involved developing closer relationships with the ASEAN member states. Globalization and regionalization are of course relative concepts; one need not be at the expense of the other. Indeed, as we will see, Singapore's recent efforts towards regionalization run parallel to its efforts to maintain links with the economies outside the region.

The discussion is divided into four parts: first, an examination of the trends in Singapore's external trade and investment to show the extent to which its economy is globalized; second, a consideration of the ways in which global trade and investment have contributed to its external and domestic security; third, an inspection of recent trends in the international economic environment which have created imperatives for greater focus on the region; and fourth, a look at manifestations of the trend towards regionalization and an evaluation of the limits to Singapore's economic and security links with the region. We will conclude that, given the differences in the interests and objectives of the ASEAN members, there are limits to the extent to which Singapore can rely upon regionalism for national security.

Globalization of Singapore's Economy

After a brief experience with protection to promote domestic industries in the early 1960s, Singapore rapidly dismantled the protectionist

Table 2.1:   Singapore's Trade, 1965–1990 (%)

	1965	1970	1975	1980	1985	1990
Total exports/GDP	101.6	81.9	95.4	171.3	130.5	151.8
Total imports/GDP	128.8	129.8	144.1	212.2	150.4	175.1
Domestic exports/GDP	25.9	31.6	56.4	106.6	84.7	100.1

Note: Does not include trade with Indonesia.
Source: Urn *et al.* 1988, p. 276; Ministry of Trade and Industry 1991.

barriers following separation from Malaysia in 1965. The few remaining import restrictions exist to serve social purposes rather than to protect domestic producers. Food, beverages and tobacco are the only products on which steep tariffs are applied for protectionist purposes.[8] Barriers to foreign investments have also been minimal. As a result of these measures, Singapore has one of the most globalized economies in the world, evident in every facet of the economy.

In the twenty years between 1970–1990, Singapore's total trade increased by more than sixteen times, from S$12.3 billion to S$205 billion (Ministry of Trade and Industry 1991). Its exports' share of total GDP increased, as shown in Table 2.1, from 101.6 percent in 1965 to 151.8 percent in 1990. Imports increased similarly, from 128.8 percent to 175.1 percent of the GDP. Because of its huge exports and imports, Singapore is the most trade-dependent nation in the world and the world's seventeenth largest trader,[9] which is truly remarkable considering its small population. Consistent with the globalization trend, Singapore's trade has shifted away from the Southeast Asian region and has become increasingly global.

---

[8] Willy Kraus and Wilfried Lutkenhorst, *The Economic Development of the Pacific Basin*, New York, St Martin's Press, 1986, p. 28.
[9] *The Economist*, "Pocket World in Figures", London; *Far Eastern Economic Review*, Review Publishing, Hong Kong, 1991, p. 28.

Table 2.2:   Destination of Singapore's Exports, 1966–1989 (%)

	1966[a]	1976	1978	1980	1982	1984	1986	1988	1989
USA	4.79	13.58	15.36	12.13	11.07	18.66	22.39	23.28	22.76
Europe	12.80[b]	13.70[b]	12.77[b]	15.26	10.58	11.88	12.69	15.08	15.49
Japan	3.65	9.47	9.28	7.69	9.59	8.71	8.23	8.44	8.35
ASEAN	40.788	27.50	24.13	25.78	33.77	28.40	24.17	23.14	23.48
Brunei	1.43	1.59	1.49	1.36	1.52	1.14	1.34	1.03	1.01
Malaysia	35.42	14.08	13.31	14.31	15.56	15.09	14.18	13.26	13.36
Philippines	0.45	1.36	1.40	1.34	1.37	0.79	1.05	1.29	1.45
Thailand	3.48	2.76	3.73	4.16	3.38	4.46	3.50	5.33	5.39
Indonesia		7.71	4.20	4.61	11.94	6.92	4.10	2.23	2.27

[a] Excludes Indonesia. [b] EC only.

Source: *Yearbook of Statistics*, Singapore, various years; International Monetary Fund, *Direction of Trade Statistics*, various years.

Tables 2.2 and 2.3 show that Singapore's trade with ASEAN has been overtaken increasingly by trade with the USA, Europe and Japan. While ASEAN has until recently been the single largest source of imports (Table 2.3), about half of these comprise entrepot activities. When entrepot imports are subtracted from total imports, Japan, USA and the European Community (EC) come out ahead of ASEAN.[10]

The international orientation of Singapore's economy is also evident in the degree to which it relies on foreign investments. Table 2.4 shows that more than four-fifths of the investments in Singapore's manufacturing since 1973 (and most likely earlier) have come from foreigners. During the 1975–1984 period, foreign-owned (more than 50 percent) firms in Singapore on average accounted for 54.6 percent of the total workforce, 72.9 percent of the total output, 84.2 percent of the manufacturing workforce and 67.2 percent of the capital expenditure in the manufacturing sector.[11] Among the foreign

---

[10] Lim Chong Yah et al., *Policy Options for the Singapore Economy*, Singapore, McGraw-Hill, 1988, p. 282.

[11] Koh Ai Tee, "Linkages and the International Environment", in Lawrence Krause et al., eds., *The Singapore Economy Reconsidered*, Singapore, Institute of Southeast Asian Studies, 1987, pp. 21–53, p. 25.

Table 2.3:   Sources of Singapore's Imports, 1966–1989 (%)

	1966[a]	1976	1978	1980	1982	1984	1986	1988	1989
USA	5.18	12.34	11.63	12.77	11.62	13.59	14.43	14.98	16.54
Europe	17.28[b]	10.15[b]	10.87[b]	12.39	11.69	11.83	14.11	14.29	14.85
Japan	11.40	14.96	17.48	16.70	16.24	17.08	19.19	21.15	20.59
ASEAN	32.928	22.73	24.06	24.76	24.75	24.16	20.42	21.67	19.35
Brunei	0.02	0.22	0.69	0.74	0.70	0.63	0.52	0.24	0.15
Malaysia	28.69	13.35	11.70	12.56	12.05	13.98	12.85	14.12	12.73
Philippines	0.23	0.38	0.46	0.28	0.33	0.60	0.70	0.58	0.53
Thailand	3.98	2.15	2.51	1.80	1.69	2.06	2.79	3.10	2.43
Indonesia		6.63	8.70	9.38	9.98	6.89	3.56	3.63	3.51

[a] Excludes Indonesia. [b]EC only.
Source: *Yearbook of Statistics*, Singapore, various years; International Monetary Fund, *Direction of Trade Statistics*, various years.

Table 2.4:   Net Investment Commitments in Manufacturing, 1973–1990

	Total ($m)	Foreign ($m)	Foreign as % of the total
1973[a]	259.9	224.1	86.2
1975[a]	306.3	246.8	80.6
1980[a]	1417.9	1199.0	84.6
1985	1120.4	888.0	79.2
1990	2484.3	2217.5	89.3

[a] Excludes petrochemicals.
Source: Ministry of Trade and Industry, *Economic Survey of Singapore*, various years.

investors, USA, Japan and European countries have accounted for nearly all the foreign investments. This is to be expected, given they are the world's most industrialized nations whose MNCs account for a large percentage of world trade and investment.

What is even more significant is that foreign investment in Singapore has been increasingly in the form of direct investment. Foreign direct investment's share of total foreign equity investment increased from 84 percent in 1970 to 93 percent in 1981; the share accounted for by portfolio investment declined correspondingly.[12] Of the total net inflow of US$13.05 billion in foreign long-term capital into Singapore during the 1975–1988 period, 86.53 percent was in the form of direct investment, 1.08 percent in portfolio investment and 12.38 percent in "other" long-term capital.[13] The distinctive feature of direct investment is that it gives control of the firm to the investor, which implies that a large proportion of Singapore's corporate sector is controlled directly by foreigners. This is in contrast to the other ASEAN members and South Korea and Taiwan, which rely mostly on portfolio investment and borrowing for foreign long-term capital.[14]

The above discussion shows clearly that Singapore's economy is highly globalized in terms of trade and investment. This has been to a large extent shaped by market forces, which themselves have been shaped by the conditions established by the state. The Singapore state has played an active role in globalizing the economy, by undertaking a range of measures. Generous fiscal incentives have been available to exporters. The Economic Expansion Incentives Act and Pioneer Industries Ordinance have provided for substantially reduced taxation on profits from manufactured exports.[15] The Employment Act and the Industrial Relations (Amendment) Act of 1968 have similarly favored investors. The former increased working hours, reduced public holidays, paid holidays, rest days and sick leave, and limited bonus payments to employees. The latter curtailed trade union rights by excluding promotions, transfers, retrenchments, dismissals, reinstatements and work assignments from collective bargaining. Strikes in essential services and sympathy strikes were already banned by statutory measures taken in 1966.[16] Measures to improve infrastructure necessary for export production included the establishment of numerous public enterprises to provide

---

[12] Lim Chong Yah *et al.*, *op. cit.*

[13] International Monetary Fund, "International Financial Statistics", Washington DC, 1990.

[14] Lim Chong Yah *et al.*, *op. cit.*, p. 251.

[15] Rodan, *op. cit.*, p. 87.

[16] *Ibid.*, pp. 91–92.

the goods and services considered necessary to make Singapore attractive to foreign investors.[17] In the late 1980s, the government offered fiscal incentives to service exports and to foreign companies to locate their regional headquarters in Singapore.

No doubt there were sound economic reasons (the neo-classical economists' admonition against state intervention in the market notwithstanding) for the state's actions. But as the following section will show, the measures were also consistent with its security needs and, as such, were an integral part of its national security strategy.

The Security Motives Underlying Globalization

In one of the most thorough discussions on the subject, Chin has argued that Singapore took measures in the following areas to reduce threats to its security: diplomacy to encourage US presence in the region; economic development and nation-building; upgrading of military capability to provide credible defense; and cultivating ties with Malaysia and Indonesia.[18] Missing in his discussion is any mention of the measures aimed at increasing Singapore's integration into the global economy to strengthen its security. This lapse is common in discussions on Singapore's national security. This is surprising given that the foreign policy framework of small states tends to emphasize foreign economic relations over political or military relations.[19] A brief look at Singapore's economic development will show that integration into the global economy has served to enhance its external as well as internal security.

---

[17] *Ibid.*, pp. 93–96.

[18] Chin Kin Wah, "Singapore: Threat Perception and Defence Spending in a City State", in Chin Kin Wah, ed., *Defence Spending in Southeast Asia*, Singapore, Institute of Southeast Asian Studies, 1987, pp. 194–223; and Derek da Cunha , "Major Asian Powers and the Development of the Singaporean and Malaysian Armed Forces", *Contemporary Southeast Asia*, vol. 13, no. 1, 1991, pp. 57–71.

[19] Maurice A. East, "Size and Foreign Policy", *World Politics*, vol. 25, July 1973, pp. 556–576.

External security

Singapore is a small state (a population of 2.7 million concentrated on 624 square km of land) faced with severe geopolitical vulnerabilities. Its establishment following a bitter row with Malaysia, together with the numerical superiority of the Chinese in a country located in a region populated by Malays, is a source of constant insecurity *vis-à-vis* its neighbors. Its insecurity is fueled further by its economic prosperity, built partly on its role as entrepot to the region, which is a source of resentment among its neighbors. Too small and weak to cope with these insecurities on its own in the years following its separation from Malaysia, Singapore had to seek support for its survival from foreign powers.

One source of external support, of course, could have been the Association of Southeast Asian Nations (ASEAN), established in 1967 following the end of confrontation between Indonesia and Malaysia. After all, if overcoming the threats posed by its neighbors was the main objective of Singapore's foreign policy, then what better mechanism could there be than a regional organization committed to promoting peace and cooperation among the member countries? But ASEAN as an organization, instead of providing a mechanism for overcoming the threats, embodied the very problems Singapore was trying to overcome.

ASEAN as a regional organization was aimed, first and foremost, at providing a mechanism for peaceful settlement of disputes among its members. But this commitment to subregional harmony was forged in response to a common fear of communism. It suppressed, but did not eliminate, lingering suspicions and animosities within ASEAN. As Prime Minister Lee Kuan Yew put it, "your best friends are never your immediate neighbors".[20] Moreover, despite the common fear of communism, the founders of ASEAN never conceived the grouping as a defense organization. Rather, ASEAN

---

[20] Lee Kuan Yew, quoted in Charles E. Morrison and Astri Suhrke, *Strategies of Survival: The Foreign Policy Dilemmas of Smaller Asian States*, Brisbane, University of Queensland Press, 1978, p. 187.

was established to promote economic growth, social progress and cultural development.[21]

While Singapore participated actively in the establishment of ASEAN, it had no illusions about the security it could expect from it. According to Morrison and Suhrke, "Singapore's misgivings stemmed from a fear that regional cooperation tended to reject large power involvement in the region without providing any real substitute for that involvement".[22] It viewed the ASEAN states as too weak to provide effective support against threats posed by Vietnam or extra-regional powers. More importantly, the organization could not be relied upon for support in times of conflict with the other member states. Singapore, however, supported ASEAN in the interest of improving relations with its neighbors and because of the psychological security that this was expected to provide, which was badly needed to build investors' confidence.[23] But it also pragmatically recognized the limitations of ASEAN in serving its security needs.

Not only did ASEAN not foster military security, it did little to promote Singapore's economic security. In fact the organization made no progress in economic cooperation until 1976. At the Bali summit that year, Singapore's proposal for a free trade area was supported only by the Philippines and bitterly opposed by Indonesia.[24] Eventually, in January 1977, the ASEAN Preferential Trading Arrangement (PTA) reducing tariffs on ASEAN imports was signed. In subsequent years, the ASEAN Industrial Complementation scheme (AIC), ASEAN Industrial Projects (AIP) and ASEAN Industrial Joint Ventures scheme (AIJV) were gradually established to expand regional economic cooperation. Researchers have been virtually unanimous in the collusion that these projects have had

---

[21] Arnfinn Jorgensen-Dahl, *Regional Organisation and Order in South-East Asia*, London, Macmillan, 1982, p. 43; Marjorie L. Suriyamongkol, *Politics of ASEAN Economic Cooperation: The Case of ASEAN Industrial Projects*, Singapore, Oxford University Press, 1988, p. 52.

[22] Morrison and Suhrke, *op. cit.*, p. 189.

[23] *Ibid.*, p. 190.

[24] Jorgensen-Dahl, *op. cit.*, pp. 55–56.

negligible impact on the ASEAN economies.[25] The reasons for the failure of these schemes include lack of complementarity of ASEAN economies, differences in stages of development and trade regimes of ASEAN countries.[26]

With little hope for military or economic security from ASEAN, Singapore had to look beyond the region to strengthen its national security. Even this was not easy. Put bluntly, Singapore had little to offer to those great powers whose presence it sought to strengthen its security. This became abundantly clear when Singapore's pleas for continued presence of British troops in Singapore failed to reverse Britain's decision to withdraw its troops in 1971. American presence was its second-best hope. But this was again a matter in which it had little bargaining power. The best that it was able to secure was the Five Power Defense Arrangements (FPDA), instituted in 1971, which committed the UK, Australia and New Zealand to defend Malaysia and Singapore against external aggression. However, the limited credibility of FPDA was immediately apparent; neither Singapore nor Malaysia viewed it as an adequate guarantee against external aggression. Moreover, while the FPDA promoted a limited degree of defense cooperation between Singapore and Malaysia, given that Malaysia and Indonesia were the main sources of threat to Singapore it is unlikely that the distant powers would have come to the latter's defense in case of serious conflict with either of its neighbors.

The inability of ASEAN to promote Singapore's military or economic security, and the latter's own inability to secure military support from great powers, left Singapore with only one option in the international arena: security through participation in the global economy. By allowing, indeed inviting, foreign participation in the economy, it created stakes for external powers to protect Singapore in order to protect their own economic interests. In other words, it internationalized Singapore's protection against foreign attack. The strategy

---

[25] Hans Christoph Rieger, "Regional Economic Cooperation in the Asia Pacific Region", *Asian-Pacific Economic Literature*, vol. 3, no. 2, 1989, pp. 5–33.

[26] *Ibid.*, p. 8.

was captured in the view of Foreign Minister S. Rajaratnam that "the world is our hinterland": "We are more than a regional city. We draw sustenance not only from the region but also from the international economic system to which as a global city we belong and which will be the final arbiter of whether we prosper or decline".[27] He then went on to claim that "an independent Singapore survives and will survive because it has established a relationship of interdependence in the rapidly expanding global economic system".

In contrast with other newly-independent states which took measures to restrict investments by MNCs, Singapore welcomed them. Apart from the immediate economic benefits such investments brought, the MNCs were viewed as a resource which their home governments would have an interest in protecting. The strategy of attracting direct investment (rather than portfolio investment or foreign loans) was especially conducive because it created direct involvement of the parent companies in Singapore's economy. If attracting foreign capital was the only objective, then Singapore could have resorted to the path followed by most developing countries — tapping foreign loans. But loans would not have nurtured the foreign companies', and their governments', commitment to the survival of the island-state to the same extent as direct investment.

Economic development and national security through openness to trade and investment was made easier by the absence of ideological opposition to Western dominance in Singapore's foreign policy outlook. Rajaratnam, in a speech in 1979, said, "Western imperialism, as we have known it, is today about as real as Roman imperialism or the other great imperialisms which now exist only in history books. Western power and influence is certainly a reality but its imperialism is no longer so".[28] Unlike other developing countries which regarded foreign investment as a threat to their sovereignty, Singapore viewed it as a resource for reducing the state's vulnerability.

---

[27] S. Rajaratnam, "Singapore: Global City", Address to the Singapore Press Club, February 6, 1972 (included in the Appendix of this book).

[28] Chan Heng Chee and Obaid ul Haq, eds., *S. Rajaratnam: The Prophetic and the Political*, Singapore, Brash, Graham, 1987.

Rapid economic growth based on export-led industrialization has also been important for the financial basis it has provided for Singapore's huge defense expenditures, which formed 29.19 percent of total public expenditures between 1976 and 1989.[29] The expenditures have enabled it to acquire some of the latest military hardware available. Its airforce has aircrafts, missiles and radar systems which are unmatched in the region.[30]

Internal security

External security through foreign trade and investment was only one side of Singapore's broader national security strategy. Singapore's leaders recognized that the survival of the country would depend not only on its protection from external aggression, but from internal unrest as well. Poverty in a multiethnic milieu formed a fertile ground for communism and communalism, which were viewed as the key threats to survival. Rapid economic development through openness to trade and investment was seen as the most effective long-term solution, which formed the basis of its foreign economic policy. It is therefore difficult to agree with the assertion that "Singapore does not require a foreign policy to serve domestic politics".[31]

Economic development through participation in the global division of labor was of course contingent upon low wages and industrial peace. These conditions were secured through stem labor laws (mentioned earlier), the acceptability of which was dependent upon a growing economy. Fortunately, the government's strategy paid off as Singapore's GNP grew on an average of 7 percent between 1965 and 1989.[32] Its real GDP grew at an annual rate of 9.0 percent during

---

[29] Asian Development Bank, "Key Indicators of Developing Asian and Pacific Countries", Manila, 1990.

[30] Tim Huxley, "Singapore and Malaysia: A Precarious Balance", *The Pacific Review*, vol. 4, no. 3, 1991, pp. 204–213, p. 211.

[31] Chan Heng Chee, "'Singapore: Domestic Structure and Foreign Policy", p. 129.

[32] World Bank, "World Development Report 1991: The Challenge of Development", Oxford, Oxford University Press, 1991.

the 1971–1980 period, and at a rate of 6.3 percent during the 1981–1990 period.[33] While it is impossible to pinpoint the contributions of foreign trade and investment to Singapore's economic growth, there is no doubt that they are substantial.

The successful pursuit of an export-industrialization strategy, and the economic benefits that this success brought to the general population, has been the People's Action Party's (PAP's) main claim to the right to unchallenged rule in Singapore. The population has continuously approved the claim, as evidenced in the landslide margins with which it has been elected in every election held since independence. The legitimacy for the regime that flowed from its successful pursuit of economic development enabled it to crush any threat to domestic stability. To the extent economic progress benefited, albeit unequally, every ethnic group, inter-ethnic conflict was dampened and national unity promoted.

Singapore's experience in securing regime legitimacy and internal security may be described as what Rosenau has called legitimacy through "performance criteria".[34] The population consented to the PAP's rule because of its performance in managing the economy. But this is by its very nature a risky strategy. As Buzan has argued, states that base their legitimacy on maximization of wealth through extensive trade are "vulnerable to disruptions in the flows of trade and finance".[35] Singapore encountered such a vulnerability in the 1980s when the global environment turned uncertain and the long-term viability of reliance on the vagaries of the global economy became doubtful. This led Singapore's leaders to pay greater attention to the region for economic and security links. The following are some of the pressures which necessitated reassessment of the earlier strategy of relying on the global economy and a move towards greater emphasis on the region.

---

[33] Asian Development Bank, "Asian Development Outlook, Asian Development Bank", 1991.

[34] James N. Rosenau, "The New Global Order: Understanding and Outcomes", Paper presented at the XVth World Congress of the International Political Science Association, Buenos Aires, 1991, p. 7.

[35] Buzan, *op. cit.*, p. 128.

Pressures for Regionalization: The Threat of Increased Protectionism

While tariff barriers to trade have declined continuously since the 1940s, non-tariff barriers maintained by the developed countries have increased somewhat since the 1970s.[36] Although the actual increase in non-tariff barriers has been small so far, Singapore cannot but be apprehensive.[37] Its dependence on exports of a narrow range of products (because of specialization) makes it especially vulnerable to protectionism in its major markets.

The USA, which is Singapore's largest export market, has been the main source of the protectionist threat. Its ballooning trade deficit with Japan and the Asian newly-industrializing countries (NICs) raised fears that the American government would act under domestic political pressures to protect its producers from imports. While no significant protectionist measure affecting Singapore has been actually adopted, in 1987 there were as many as 150 trade bills providing for various kinds of protection before the Congress.[38] What is significant in Singapore's case is not the actual establishment of barriers to its exports, but that it must be prepared for the possibility that such a measure might be adopted.

Singapore's policy-makers also cannot but be apprehensive of the ongoing negotiations to establish the North American Free Trade Area (NAFTA). The elimination of barriers to trade and investment will make Mexico a formidable competitor for foreign investments because of its cheap labor and its proximity to the US market. It is feared that investments in Mexico will be at the expense of East and Southeast Asia.

The future trade and investment policies of the EC have been another source of concern. The EC was committed to establishing, by

---

[36] Bela Balassa and Carol Balassa, "Industrial Protection in the Developed Countries", *The World Economy*, vol. 7, June 1984, pp. 179–196.

[37] Ministry of Trade and Industry, Singapore, *The Singapore Economy: New Directions*, Report of the Economic Committee, 1986.

[38] Development Bank of Singapore, "US Trade Protectionism — Implications for Singapore and other NICs", Report no. 13, Singapore, 1987, p. 1.

December 31, 1992, "an area without internal frontiers in which the free movement of goods, persons, services and capital is ensured". The market will comprise over 320 million people and a total GNP of US$4.3 trillion, which will form the largest market in the world.[39] The concern is that while dismantling internal barriers, the EC may erect new barriers to exporters outside the community. The retaliatory power of the strengthened EC would also be immense as it would be able to demand concessions which few countries would have the capacity to resist. The integration of East European economies into the EC will especially hurt countries such as Singapore. Their cheap labor and proximity to West European markets make them attractive investment sites. Decision-makers in ASEAN states see greater regional economic cooperation as a way of offsetting the adverse effects of European integration.

The future of the Uruguay Round of GATT negotiations is also a cause for concern. The negotiations were scheduled to end in December 1990, but were extended because of a stalemate over agricultural subsidies and liberalized trade in services. While unable to affect the course of negotiations, Singapore cannot escape their outcomes. The fear is that break-down of the negotiations will lead to collapse of the liberal global trading environment and a shift towards bilateralism and inward-looking trade blocs. As the then Deputy and now Prime Minister, Goh Chok Tong, remarked, if "others are forming trading arrangements, if GATT talks fail and Japan-US talks break down, then there is no choice but for us to look after our own interests by following what others do".[40]

Doubts about long-term viability of the globalization strategy

There is a fear that in the long-run, Singapore cannot sustain its record of economic growth based on export-oriented industrialization. The shortage of land and labor is bound to increase business costs and

---

[39] *Economic Bulletin 1989*, "An Integrated European Market in 1992: Implications for Singapore", vol. 18, March 1989, pp. 11–16, p. 11.

[40] Goh Chok Tong, *The Straits Times*, March 5, 1991.

reduce Singapore's attractiveness to foreign investors. Rents have increased rapidly, by 30–40 percent per year between 1986 and 1990, and now Singapore has one of the highest rates of office rents in the world. Similarly, wages have increased in real terms on average by 6.2 percent annually between 1981 and 1990. It is feared that investments in manufacturing will be less forthcoming because of their diversion to other developing countries with lower costs. Another worrying trend is the shift in comparative advantage caused by advances in microelectronics. Since the 1980s, many MNCs have shut down their overseas plants and moved back home because automated production processes have reduced their demand for labor and the need for locating their production in low-wage countries. According to Goh Chok Tong, "New technology, the microchip revolution and robotic slaves that do not go on strike for better pay and working conditions have relieved the pressures on American, European and Japanese companies to seek sanctuaries outside their home".[41]

Uncertainties also surround the service sector, which was targeted as the sector with the brightest future not too long ago. Advances in information technology are expected to reduce demand for middle managers in certain service sectors, turning these sectors into low-waged and unskilled employment ghettos. This will occur at a time when Singapore's population has become used to seeing real improvements in its economic well-being. It is hoped that other economies in the region will absorb some of these professionals.

The end of the Cold War

The end of the Cold War has had a mixed impact on Singapore's economic security predicament. On the one hand, it has brightened the outlook for security and stability in the Asia-Pacific region, thereby improving the conditions for regional economic development and trade. On the other hand, it threatens the privileged market access granted by the USA to East and Southeast Asian countries for their

---

[41] Goh Chok Tong, in Rodan, *Singapore Changes Guard*, p. 197.

pro-Western stance in the Cold War rivalry. As Lee Kuan Yew warned: "Now the race between Democracy and Communism has been won and done with. The industrial countries no longer need to woo the developing countries with concessions to win their allegiance and to prove the superiority of democracy plus the free market. So it may be more difficult for the future NICs".[42]

With the East-West hostility now over, it is feared that developed countries will deal with their trading partners on the principle of strict reciprocity and will not offer trade concessions in return for support for their military objectives. Evidence of this trend is discernible in the ongoing Uruguay Round of GATT negotiations where developing countries are under intense pressure to remove trade barriers and to respect intellectual property rights in return for maintaining their access to the developed countries' markets. There are also moves to designate Singapore and other Asian NICs as developed countries, which will lead to withdrawal of many concessions they currently enjoy as developing countries.

Expanding economic opportunities in the region

This is one of the fastest-growing regions in the world and there are plenty of economic opportunities right here. The average annual real economic growth in ASEAN in the 1980s was over 6 percent and the 1990s are expected to show a continuation of the trend. So the earlier belief that only the industrialized nations could provide the economic opportunities sought by Singapore is changing. In particular, new opportunities in exporting services to the region are perceived.[43] Singapore is the third largest exporter of services in the Asia-Pacific,[44] and its firms are well-placed to take advantage of

---

[42] Lee Kuan Yew, "Asia-Pacific Region in the New Geopolitical Context", Keynote Address at the Informal Gathering of the World Economic Leaders, February 1990.

[43] Ministry of Trade and Industry, *op. cit.*

[44] Chung H. Lee and Seiji Naya, "Patterns of Trade and Investment in Services in the Asia-Pacific Region", in Chung H. Lee and Seiji Naya, eds., *Trade and Investment in Services in the Asia-Pacific Region*, Boulder, Colorado, Westview Press, 1988, p. 34.

the opportunities that will arise in the region if the Uruguay Round succeeds in removing barriers to trade in services.

Regionalization and Its Limits

Three recent developments indicate a trend towards regionalization in Singapore's economic strategy. The first is the launching of the Growth Triangle concept in December 1989. The Growth Triangle seeks to promote economic development in the region by taking advantage of the differences in factor endowments of Singapore, Johor in Malaysia and Riau in Indonesia. The first is strongly placed to provide capital, technology and infrastructural support, and the other two have abundant land and labor to offer. It is hoped that investors will be attracted to take advantage of the complete package of low wages, high skills and solid infrastructure offered by the region.

Second, Singapore's long-standing objective of establishing free trade among ASEAN appears closer than ever before to realization. After years of debate, in January 1992 ASEAN leaders decided to establish an ASEAN Free Trade Area (AFTA). The agreement would gradually eliminate all tariffs on manufactured products over a fifteen-year period. Studies done recently at the East-West Center in Hawaii show that complete elimination of ASEAN tariffs would substantially increase the share of Singapore's exports to ASEAN. Indeed, its exporters will benefit from the arrangement more than those of its trading partners. So if the AFTA is actually implemented, the regional orientation of Singapore's economy will increase substantially in the long-run.

Third, Singapore's leaders are also paying greater attention to the exploitation of economic opportunities in Indochina. Despite its ban on investment in Vietnam, Singapore is the latter's third largest trading partner, after the (former) Soviet Union and Japan.[45] Once normalcy returns to Cambodia and economic liberalization has advanced sufficiently in Vietnam and Laos, Singapore's trade with these countries is expected to grow tremendously.

---

[45] *Far Eastern Economic Review,* June 27, 1991.

However, there are limits to Singapore's efforts to regionalize the bases of its economy and security. To begin with, ASEAN is too small — its total GDP forms only 2 percent of world GDP — to be an alternative to the global economy. The USA, Europe, Japan and the other NICs will continue to be its main economic partners in the foreseeable future.

Equally importantly, the neighbors' different security objectives will continue to undermine the establishment of a regional security order, regardless of the perceived need for it.

Singapore's trade relations with the region have witnessed a secular decline despite efforts at the political level to promote ASEAN economic cooperation. ASEAN as a destination for Singapore's exports declined from 27.5 percent in 1976 to 23.5 percent in 1989, and as a source of imports from 32.92 percent to 19.35 percent during the period 1966–1989 (Tables 2.2 and 2.3). While Singapore's intra-industry manufacturing trade with the ASEAN partners increased from 41.7 percent of its total manufacturing trade in 1970 to 46.7 percent in 1981, the level of increase was insignificant compared to a more than doubling of its intra-industry trade with the EC, Japan and the USA during the same period.[46] The region's share of Singapore's trade is likely to decline even further as the neighboring countries develop their economies and reduce their reliance on its entrepot facilities. So Singapore's efforts to promote stronger links with the region will have to be balanced by efforts to maintain its global links.

Indeed, it is doubtful if the AFTA will yield the level of benefits mentioned earlier. Studies showing increased trade and investments are premised on substantial reductions in trade barriers, which is clearly not the case. The agreement would take fifteen years to be implemented fully, would allow members to opt out of tariff reduction and would exclude trade in agricultural products and services. The exclusion of the latter is especially significant considering Singapore's objective of becoming a regional center for service exports. It is also likely that its trading partners would resort

---

[46] Mohamed Ariff and Hal Hill, *Export-Oriented Industrialisation: The ASEAN ASEAN*, Sydney & Boston, Allen & Unwin, 1985, p. 207.

frequently to opting out of tariff reductions on products of which it is the main supplier because of the unequal benefits that would otherwise accrue to the island-state.

Singapore's efforts to strengthen bilateral economic links with Malaysia and Indonesia are also problematic. Its aim of becoming a high-technology manufacturing center and regional service center runs counter to the neighbors' economic nationalism.[47] The Malaysian government's delisting of Malaysian stocks in Singapore in 1988 and the efforts of Indonesia and Malaysia to refine their own petroleum are undoubtedly motivated by economic nationalism. There is also resentment in the neighboring countries to the idea, embodied in the Growth Triangle, that Johor and Riau are Singapore's hinterland providing cheap labor and land. The youth wing of the ruling party in Malaysia has already criticized the growing Singaporean presence in Johor's economy. Besides, ASEAN members see economic cooperation as a zero-sum game. At an ASEAN conference in 1987, the Malaysian Prime Minister observed, "It is axiomatic that one person's loss is another person's gain".[48] Since Singapore is the most developed country in the region, there will always be fear that any economic arrangement would benefit it disproportionately. This attitude has been one of the main stumbling blocks to economic cooperation in the past and will continue to be so in the foreseeable future.

Economic constraints apart, there are a number of uncertainties and challenges in the regional security environment which might undermine prospects for greater regionalism in Singapore's economic strategy. Perhaps the most serious factor here is the state of Singapore's bilateral political and security relations with Malaysia and Indonesia. On the positive side, Singapore has sought and secured closer defense cooperation with these two neighbors, as indicated in the growing number of bilateral military exercises.

---

[47] Hans H. Indorf, *Impediments to Regionalism in Southeast Asia*, Singapore, Institute of Southeast Asian Studies, 1984, pp. 48–64.
[48] Mahathir Mohammed, quoted in Rieger, "Regional Economic Co-operation in the Asia Pacific Region", p. 20.

Singapore and Indonesia have been conducting bilateral naval exercises since 1974, air exercises since 1980, and land exercises since 1989. Bilateral naval and air exercises have been carried out with Malaysia since 1984 and land exercises since 1989.[49] While the scope of the bilateral military exercises is still narrow, the fact that they are held at all is no small achievement given the countries' historical suspicions of each other.

But the scope for fundamental improvements in Singapore's security ties with Indonesia and Malaysia is limited. While defense ties contribute to regional confidence-building, they are insufficient to overcome divergent threat perceptions and security objectives. Malaysia and Indonesia's continued adherence to regional non-alignment runs counter to Singapore's emphasis on securing a strong American military umbrella in the region. This has thus far prevented consensus on a regional security framework for the post-Cold War era. Moreover, Singapore's political relations with Malaysia remain delicate and vulnerable to periodic strains. Recent examples include the controversy caused by the visit of the Israeli President to Singapore, Malaysia's initial unhappiness over Singapore's offer of military facilities to the USA, and the suspension of bilateral military exercises over a spying incident. Territorial disputes between Malaysia and Singapore (over Horsborough Lighthouse, for example) and between Malaysia and Indonesia over islands off the northeast coast of Sabah are also important factors in assessing the prospects for regionalism in Singapore's economic strategy.

Economic cooperation with Indonesia and Malaysia is also contingent upon the continuity of leadership in these countries. The PAP leaders, who have developed a working relationship with the leaders in Malaysia and Indonesia over the years, are concerned about the retirement of the current generation of leaders and their replacement by those who might be hostile to Singapore. Lee Kuan Yew on numerous occasions has spoken glowingly of Mahathir and Suharto. To quote him, "No event has had a more profound influence on the

---

[49] Bilveer Singh, "Singapore, Malaysia and Indonesia Triangular Defence Pact: Potentials and Perils", *Asia Defence Journal*, December 1990, pp. 4–6, p. 5.

development of the region than the character and outlook of President Suharto of Indonesia".[50] Singapore's leaders and press made little secret of their preference for Barisan during recent elections in Malaysia and appear to be doing the same for the coming presidential election in Indonesia.[51]

The Singapore government's continued emphasis on a strong national military deterrent is a reflection of its lingering insecurity *vis-à-vis* its neighbors, as well as a source of suspicion in its bilateral relations with them. The proclaimed reason for this is the need to protect against extra-regional powers which might threaten Singapore's security. As the then Defense Minister (now Deputy Prime Minister) Lee Hsien Loong argued, "Southeast Asia being what it is, trouble may break out suddenly, so we have to be prepared. Other states are also acquiring the capability to project power into the region".[52] He was presumably referring to China, Japan and India, which the government believes harbor ambitions to dominate the region. It has been argued, however, that the real reason for the Republic's military preparedness has little to do with extra-regional threats and is more directly addressed to the perceived threats posed by its immediate neighbor.[53] Singapore's continued reliance on extra-regional security guarantees, as well as its continued emphasis on national military deterrence capability, underscore the limits of regionalism in promoting Singapore's security.

The limitations to regionalism noted above have led Singapore to balance its regionalization efforts with globalism. This was evident in its participation in the launching of the Asia-Pacific Economic Cooperation (APEC) in 1989 and hosting of the ministerial meeting in the following year. Singapore does not fully share Malaysia's and Indonesia's suspicion that APEC might lead to the dilution of ASEAN. Its Minister for Trade and Industry argued that "to us, ASEAN and

[50] *The Straits Times*, April 17, 1986.

[51] Hari Singh and Suresh Naraynan, "Changing Dimensions in Malaysian Politics: The Johor Bahru By-Election", *Asian Survey*, vol. 29, no. 5, 1990, pp. 514–529, p. 524.

[52] Lee Hsien Loong, in da Cunha, "Major Asian Powers and the Development of the Singaporean and Malaysian Armed Forces", p. 60.

[53] Huxley, *op. cit.*

APEC are really concentric circles to which we belong. They have different processes, they have different memberships".[54] Singapore's leaders view APEC as an organization which can serve as a useful tool to lower trade barriers. As the Minister put it, "APEC will be a useful informal group, for the purposes of the GATT Uruguay Round, of like-minded countries with a common interest in a successful outcome of the Round".[55] Thus, Singapore seeks to strengthen its ASEAN ties without weakening its links with the global economy.

The Singapore government's cautious attitude towards the East Asia Economic Grouping (EAEG) proposed by Malaysia in December 1990 also indicates a similar effort to balance regionalism with globalism. The initial reaction was to support Malaysia without antagonising the USA, which opposed the proposal for the fear that EAEG might eventually lead to the establishment of an East Asian trading bloc. When US opposition continued despite efforts to allay its fears, Singapore played a key role at the meeting of ASEAN economic ministers, held in October 1991, in diluting the proposal. It was finally agreed at the meeting that the grouping will be called East Asia Economic Caucus (EAEC) and will serve as a forum to "discuss issues of common concern to East Asian economies".[56]

In addition to ensuring close economic links with the USA, measures have been taken to ensure the former's continued military presence in the region. In November 1990, Singapore signed a Memorandum of Understanding on Increased Use of Singapore's Military Facilities with the USA which provides for increased use of maintenance and repair facilities that have been used by the US Navy for more than 25 years.[57] The government views the agreement as "a way of tying the US more firmly to Singapore as a form of insurance".[58] While regional defense cooperation will continue, so will dependence on the USA.

---

[54] *PEER*, August 4, 1989.

[55] Lee Hsien Loong, Speech before the Indonesia Forum, Jakarta, July 11, 1990.

[56] *PEER*, October 24, 1991.

[57] Singh, "American Military Facilities in Singapore", p. 17.

[58] *PEER*, December 13, 1990.

Conclusion

This chapter inquired into the economic foundations of Singapore's security. It found that one of the most important ways in which the Republic has reduced its geostrategic vulnerability in Southeast Asia is in opening up its economy to Western trade and investment. The Western investors' presence in the Island's economy created economic stakes for them and their governments in the survival of Singapore. However, the wisdom of relying so extensively on the global economy for survival became doubtful because of global and regional political-economic developments. Since the early 1980s, uncertainties have surrounded the continued openness of the world economy. At the same time, greater opportunities have emerged for Singapore within the region. In recent years, states in the region have lowered their barriers to trade and investment and experienced economic growth rates which make them offer economic opportunities that in the past were available only in the West. As a result, the Singapore leadership has made efforts to strengthen economic and security links with regional neighbors.

However, Singapore's efforts towards regionalization are not at the expense of its globalization strategy. The structure of its economy is such that the regional economy cannot serve as a substitute for the global economy. What its regionalization efforts signify is that, unlike the 1960s and 1970s when Singapore almost single-mindedly pursued globalism, it is now making a concerted effort to strike a balance between globalism and regionalism. Regionalization is a complement to globalization, an insurance against uncertainties in the global economic environment. Balancing global and regional economic links serves Singapore's interests well and appears to be an essential feature of its current economic and security strategy.

Part II

ADAPTATIONS

3

Diplomacy in Hard Times: Singapore Confronts Global Terrorism and Regional Regression[1]

Introduction

Few countries are more sensitive to shifts in the international economic and strategic environment in formulating their foreign policy than Singapore. Integration into the global economy is a key pillar of Singapore's prosperity. Its strategic perceptions and policies are heavily conditioned by the balance of power in the international system. As such, the year 2001 was a particularly challenging time for Singapore. The global economic outlook worsened with the slowdown in the US economy. This in turn aggravated the ongoing (since 1997) regional economic crisis and produced what was officially acknowledged to be the most severe economic challenge facing Singapore since its independence. Then came the September 11 terrorist attacks on the US and the US counterstrike

[1] This chapter was originally presented as a paper at the Singapore Perspectives 2002 Conference, organized by the Institute of Policy Studies, Singapore, January 16, 2002 and appears as a chapter in Chang Li Lin, ed., *2002 Perspectives on Singapore*, Singapore, Times Academic Press and Institute of Policy Studies, 2002. Valuable research assistance for this paper was provided by Tan Ban Seng of the Institute of Defence and Strategic Studies, Singapore.

against the Taliban regime in Afghanistan. These were defining moments of the international security environment of the new millennium.

In this paper, I examine how Singapore's foreign policy responded to the shifting international and regional strategic and economic environment. The first part looks at the implications of the September 11 events. The second part focuses particularly on Singapore's efforts to address its economic (and strategic) vulnerabilities through a mix of regional, inter-regional and bilateral cooperation.

Responding to September 11: *Realpolitik* with Reason

The terrorist attacks on the World Trade Center in New York and the Pentagon in Washington, DC on September 11, 2001 and the US counterstrike against the Taliban regime in Afghanistan, were clearly the most important geopolitical events of the past year. Four aspects of their impact on international order are particularly noteworthy.

First, more than any previous episode, the September 11 attacks have demonstrated the vulnerability of nations to the new danger of transnational terrorism. One of the most succinct descriptions of the shape and magnitude of this danger came from Singapore's Minister for Trade and Industry, George Yeo, in the following words:

> The new terrorism is of a different genre. Like in a civil war, the threat is harder to pinpoint because it is within. Families may be split with the "good" and the "bad" mixed together. It is globalised by the same technologies which created the global economy. It does not consist of guerillas sheltering in the countryside making occasional incursions into the cities, but operates and draws strengths in multi-ethnic and multi-religious urban environments. It makes use of air travel and the internet. It uses similar encryption algorithms to hide its internal communications. Worst of all, its members are prepared to die for their cause.[2]

---

[2] George Yeo, "S'pore a Free Port But Will Give No Quarter to Terrorism", *The Straits Times*, October 12, 2001, p. 1.

By striking at the heart of US economic and military power, the September 11 attacks became a defining moment of international relations. They ended forever America's sense of relative invulnerability to foreign non-nuclear attacks. While terrorists had targeted American lives and assets before, few had expected attacks of such magnitude to succeed on American soil.

Second, the aftermath of September 11 demonstrated the overwhelming American dominance of the global military balance. Before it started, many experts had opined that the war against the Taliban could not be won and should not be fought. How could the US win a war in which the target was so elusive and unidentifiable? Didn't Afghanistan have a history of humiliating foreign powers?

Yet Afghanistan offered a resounding demonstration of the "new American way of war". This way of war relies on three key instruments. The first is weapon systems that can be deployed at extremely long ranges. The second is the capacity of such weapons to hit targets with extreme precision. Third and most important, is the ability of US forces to process and use an immense amount of targeting information collected on the ground, in the air and from space.[3]

In this type of warfighting, airpower, backed by target-spotting special forces, surveillance aircraft and imaging satellites with electronic systems and sensors able to peer through darkness and clouds, play a decisive role.[4] This new American way of war is also thoroughly "smart". In the 1991 Gulf War, only 10 percent of the bombs were precision-guided, meaning they could sense and hit targets from a laser beam or pick up signals from a Global Positioning System (GPS) satellite. In the Afghan War, 90 percent of the bombs were thus capable. The main precision-guided weapon in the Gulf War was a cruise missile costing US$1 million apiece. In Afghanistan, the main weapon of the air war was a kit, called Joint Direct Attack

---

[3] Thomas E. Ricks, "High-Tech Successes Point to a Sea Change in U.S. Military Thinking", *International Herald Tribune*, December 3, 2001, p. 5.

[4] The Afghanistan campaign involved the first effective use of remotely piloted surveillance aircraft ("Predators") which could beam back video pictures in real time showing enemy movements and pinpoint targets. This enabled US to hit even small elusive targets with smart bombs and guided weapons.

Munition, which could make dumb bombs smart by attaching a GPS and tail fins to guide a bomb 16 kilometers from the aircraft to the target. It came at a cost of US$18,000.[5]

But caution is warranted in drawing lessons about the US military prowess from the Afghan experience. Afghanistan had no forest cover, and the Taliban had no air defense. Its demise would mostly have been less swift but for the ruthless ground campaign of the Northern Alliance. The US might not enjoy these advantages in other theaters of conflict, such as in East Asia, where Singapore's security interests are more directly engaged.

A third aspect of international relations since September 11 has been the Bush administration's limited and selective pursuit of multi-lateralism. Dashing initial hopes and calls for a renewed commitment to multilateralism, George W. Bush did not replicate the "New World Order" approach that his father had employed against Saddam Hussein in 1990. Instead of collective security, the US invoked the right of national self-defense under the UN charter to bypass direct Security Council authorization for the conduct of the military campaign. Learning from Kosovo where alliance warfare had proven cumbersome, the US also shunned NATO's direct involvement, although the alliance had invoked its collective defense provision for the first time in history in support of the US. While the international community was generally supportive of the US position, each of America's key regional allies have demanded and secured something in return for

---

[5] Ricks, *op. cit.* Equipped with precision-guided heavy bombs that rely on all-weather targeting by satellites, US B-52s were able to destroy targets with a single payload, which would have normally required several runs. With these and other assets (including laser designators to guide smart bombs), a few hundred US troops on the ground could pinpoint targets accurately enough with a small number of bombers flying from aircraft carriers 1000 miles away or from Diego Garcia located even further away. The use of "daisy-cutters", huge 680-kg bombs that set off fuel explosions to ignite all the oxygen in an area of the size of several football fields, symbolized the massive firepower of the US, boosted the morale of the local allies and destroyed Taliban's hiding areas in remote mountain caves. See also Joseph Fitchett, "Campaign Proves the Length of U.S. Military Arm", *International Herald Tribune*, November 19, 2001.

their backing for the US. China and Russia were quick to press for an American understanding that domestic insurgencies should be viewed as a terrorist, rather than human rights issue. India secured American backing for its own war against terrorism involving Pakistani-supported Kashmir militants.

Fourth, the war in Afghanistan has introduced new uncertainties in East Asia's strategic balance. South Asia now has a much higher profile in US strategic calculations. This might affect American attention to Southeast Asia, although there are signs of increased US support to its Southeast Asian allies against the terrorist menace. The war produced a nominal improvement in Great Power relations. But here too seeds of discord were already evident. The warmth in US-Russian relations sparked by Putin's sympathy and support for the US did not prevent a mad dash to Afghanistan by Russian troops soon after its liberation from the Taliban.

The war affects China's position in several important ways. Beijing could not have been happy with the haste with which the Japanese government pushed through legislation to enable its navy (in a supporting role) to enter the waters of the Indian Ocean for the first time since the Second World War. The terrorist attacks diverted attention from Sino-US tensions, eased by China's support, albeit qualified, for the US anti-terrorist campaign. But China's sense of military vulnerability in the Taiwan Straits could only be aggravated by the awesome display of US power projection in Afghanistan. Closer US ties with both India and Pakistan are also unnerving to Beijing, as its lessens Pakistan's dependence on China while strengthening India's hand at a time when New Delhi has gained significant influence in Afghanistan through the ascendancy of its Northern Alliance allies. South Asia is no longer a separate security complex when it comes to assessing the power balance in East Asia, and this vindicates Singapore's strategy of engaging India in regional multilateral forums.

The September 11 attacks have been seen by one school of thought as proof of Samuel Huntington's thesis regarding an impending clash of civilizations. A competing view is that the attacks signify a clash *within* a civilization (Islam). In reality, both perspectives are flawed, although the second view has greater merit. Not only did governments of the world close ranks against the threat of transnational terrorism; domestic cohesion in multiethnic countries (such as Indonesia, Malaysia and Singapore) has also stood up to the challenge. In Southeast Asia, ASEAN's unity has not suffered as a result of the September 11 attacks, despite the clear religious and ethnic diversity that exists among its members. All this might not be sufficient to drown out traditional geopolitical rivalry between, or cultural conflict within, nations. But the international response to September 11 offers compelling evidence that this was no clash of civilizations.[6]

This outcome helped Singapore in formulating its own response to the September 11 attacks. For a country obsessed with vulnerability-reduction, September 11 was a major wake-up call. The government quickly reminded citizens of Singapore's past brush with terrorism, such as the Laju Ferry hijacking by the Japanese Red Army of 1974 and the skyjacking of a Singapore Airlines flight (SQ 007) by Pakistani militants in 1991. Terrorist groups remained active in Singapore's neighborhood, such as the Abu Sayyaf in the Philippines, Laskar Jihad in Indonesia and the Kumpulan Mujahideen in Malaysia, which had links with Middle East groups. Defense Minister Tony Tan pointed out that, "These are problems which worry many of our neighbouring countries and that's not very far away".[7] The discovery and arrest in December of 15 suspected terrorists (some reportedly having Al-Qaeda connections and trained in Afghanistan) showed that such concerns were hardly misplaced. Singapore, hosting important military facilities for the US and serving as a regional financial and industrial hub, presented itself as an attractive target for the Al-Qaeda terrorist network.

Singapore's immediate response to the September 11 attacks and the US strike against the Taliban was shaped by potentially conflicting impulses. On the one hand, it needed to show unequivocal support for its most important strategic partner that had suffered the

---

[6] Amitav Acharya, "Clash of Civilizations? No, of National Interests and Principles", *International Herald Tribune*, January 10, 2001, p. 8.
[7] *The Straits Times*, October 1, 2001.

biggest killing of its citizens on home soil. Yet, Singapore's leaders also had to ensure that support for the US did not cause domestic and regional strife by provoking anger among Islamic groups who might see the War Against Terrorism as a War Against Islam. This dilemma was clearly articulated by Prime Minister Goh Chok Tong at a National Stadium gathering to remember the victims of September 11. Goh acknowledged that by siding with America, Singapore "will have domestic and regional sensitivities to manage", but "[w]e must accept risks for the sake of a better world".[8]

Three aspects of Singapore's reaction to the events since September 11 are noteworthy. The first was its prompt and unequivocal condemnation of the September 11 attacks and unqualified support for the US right to retaliate. Its leaders did not blame the terrorist attacks on the US Middle East policy. A limited exception to this might have been Lee Kuan Yew's hint that the US Middle East policy has not been popular with the people of the region. (Mr Lee also advised the US to build a broad coalition that would include not just NATO members, but also Muslim and Third World countries.)[9] Nor did Singapore make its support for the US strike against Taliban conditional upon US strategic restraint in Afghanistan or economic aid. It explicitly recognized the US right to self-defense under Article 51 of the UN Charter.[10] While material help from Singapore was neither asked nor offered, the government offered to share with

---

[8] *The Straits Times*, October 24, 2001.

[9] *The Business Times*, September 20, 2001.

[10] Singapore's official position on the US strike on Afghanistan was outlined in a statement by its Permanent Representative to the UN, Kishore Mahbubani:

> "All countries have an inherent right of self-defense. The military action by the US and its coalition partners against Afghanistan is in conformity with UNSC resolution 1368 of September 13. It is a legitimate act of self-defense under Article 51 of the UN Charter.
>
> The Singapore government also supports the global campaign against terrorism, including military actions by the US and its coalition partners.
>
> Singapore is pleased to note that President Bush has made clear that the attacks are targeted only at terrorists and those who aid them.

the US information and intelligence about terrorist groups in the region and cooperate on restricting their financial mobility.[11]

But Singapore's leaders also took pains to explain to their domestic audience that support for the US was in the national interest. As B.G. Lee asserted, Singapore's anti-terrorism stance was "for our own interests", and not merely because Singapore was "a supporter of the United States".[12] If terrorism gained ground, then Singapore, a free port dependent on open trade and the global economy, will "not survive — much less prosper".[13]

A second aspect of Singapore's response to September 11 was quick adjustments to its security posture. The "traditional division of security threats into external and internal threats", declared Defense Minister Tony Tan, "no longer held" in the aftermath of September 11.[14] Singapore needed a concept of "homeland security", with the goal of "fighting low-intensity and terrorist threats, whether in the form of bombs, chemical attacks or bioterrorism".[15] Confirming Singapore's preparedness against anthrax incidents, Home Affairs Minister Wong Kan Seng stated that civil defense preparedness in the country had

---

This is a fight between the people who stand for civilized society and those out to destroy it. This is not a fight against Islam. This is also not a fight against the Afghan people as the consideration for humanitarian concerns shows.

The military action of October 7 is an immediate response that was needed. But the task does not end there. To succeed, the driving figures of international terrorism need to be rooted out and their networks comprehensively destroyed.

As a responsible member of the international community, Singapore will continue to do its part in this global efforts to eradicate terrorism."

Singapore's permanent representative Kishore Mahbubani, at the United Nations Security Council Informal Meeting on military action in Afghanistan. Source: Dow Jones Interactive, http://ptg.djnr.com/, downloaded on October 16, 2001.

[11] *The Straits Times*, October 22, 2001.
[12] *The Business Times*, October 2, 2001.
[13] *Ibid.*
[14] *The Straits Times*, November 5, 2001.
[15] *Ibid.*

"taken on a new reality for everyone after the September 11 attacks".[16] The provision of facilities to US forces renders Singapore a potential terrorist target, a danger highlighted in the arrests in December of suspected terrorists linked to the bin Laden network. The government also adopted a series of anti-terrorist measures through legislation in response to a legally-binding UN resolution passed on September 28. These measures included provisions about the freezing of terrorist funds, exchanging information about terrorist whereabouts, restricting their travel, a policy of not sheltering them, and cooperating in their prosecution.[17]

While Singapore's response to September 11 was primarily motivated by the objective of ensuring its own safety from terrorist attacks, the government did take into account the possible implications of the terrorist attacks for domestic ethnic harmony. Through statements made at the UN and at home emphasizing that acts of terrorism had nothing to do with Islam, the government tried to address the concerns of the domestic Muslim community. One day after the terrorist attacks, Ahmad Magad, an MP for Pasir Ris, stated, "Hopefully this is not a Muslim group. If it's a Muslim group that did this, we must condemn this... Islam certainly would not tolerate such an act. By any proportions, it's wrong for any religion to commit an act of this sort. It's certainly inappropriate to link this with the religion of Islam at all".[18] Senior Muslim political leaders in the country, who had been initially cautious in making any pronouncements on the subject, came up with strong condemnation of the attacks and argued that they not be seen as reflecting Islamic principles in any way. Cabinet minister George Yeo urged the US and its coalition partners to "make it very clear to the world that this is a war against Osama bin Laden and against terrorism, not a war against Islam".[19]

---

[16] *The Straits Times*, October 22, 2001.
[17] *The Straits Times*, October 6, 2001.
[18] *The Straits Times*, September 13, 2001.
[19] *The Straits Times*, October 11, 2001.

Regionalism and Inter-regionalism: Engagement with Interest

Although the year 2001 will be remembered for the terrorist attacks and the war against terrorism, other issues had already posed major foreign policy challenges for Singapore. Foremost among them was the continuing political and strategic fallout from the Asian economic crisis that began in 1997. Despite signs of recovery in 1999–2000, the economic and political outlook for the region remained bleak and uncertain, especially with the persisting instability in Indonesia. In 2001, hopes for a long-term recovery were dashed, and this time, Singapore's own economic prospects came under serious stress. This was a result not just of the weaknesses of its ASEAN neighbors, but also of the downturn in the US economy and the growing competitive strength of China, which affected Singapore's comparative advantage.

The state of play of multilateral institutions is a good barometer of the overall external environment within which Singapore's foreign policy-makers have to operate. Conventional accounts of Singapore's foreign policy framework have identified a quintessentially *realpolitik* approach, founded upon an enduring belief in the efficacy of power-balancing.[20] Yet, such accounts understate the extent to which multi-lateralism has come to occupy an important place in Singapore's foreign policy thinking and approach. Multilateralism and regionalism are not just a sideshow; at a minimum, they have offered an avenue for Singapore to pursue an enlightened self-interest, thereby becoming important foundations of Singapore's foreign policy. Contrary to conventional wisdom, Singapore's commitment to mul-tilateralism at the global and regional level has endured through "hard times", when the temptation to defect from cooperative regimes and institutions might have been especially strong.

This interest in multilateralism explains Singapore's decision to seek, successfully, a non-permanent seat in the UN Security Council. Singapore was elected for the first time as a non-permanent member

---

[20] Michael Leifer, *Singapore's Foreign Policy: Coping with Vulnerability*, London, Routledge, 2000.

of the UN Security Council at the 55th Session of the UN General Assembly on October 10, 2000. While Foreign Minister Jayakumar reminded Singaporeans that this did not mean Singapore had "arrived" on the international scene and that by virtue of being a small state, its contributions would be "small",[21] a seat in the Security Council did offer an opportunity for Singapore to raise its diplomatic profile and influence the debate on the crucial issue of Security Council reform, especially for greater transparency and clear-cut formal rules.[22] As President of the Security Council, Singapore's Permanent Representative Kishore Mahbubani chose the theme of the role of troop-contributing countries in peacekeeping operations on which to generate a debate. This led to a fruitful session between the Troop-Contributing Countries (TCCs) and the P5, where the latter were made aware of the former group's wishes for more consultation and feedback *during* the course of the UNPKO. As result of the debate, a Working Group on Peacekeeping was established. This is in addition to the active anti-terrorism stance that Singapore took after the September 11 attacks.

If regional and international institutions are mere "adjuncts" to power-balancing as the realists claim, why do so many countries invest so much effort and resources into creating, recreating and sustaining them? This question may be asked particularly of Singapore, which has a reputation for not wasting resources on ventures that promise little return and for cutting its losses when the first signs of a non-performing investment emerge. And Singapore is not only a major exponent of regionalism, it is also probably the most articulate advocate in the world today of what might be called *inter-regionalism*. Singapore sees its engagement in regional and inter-regional forums as a useful tool for advancing its economic

---

[21] http://www.singapore-window.org/sw00/001011af.htm.

[22] Kishore Mahbubani, Statement on "Agenda Item 49: Question of Equitable Representation on and Increase in the Membership of the Security Council", http://app.internet.gov.sg/scripts/mfa/pr/read_content.asp?View,1087; and Mahbubani, Speech on Road Maps and Road Blocks, November 19, 2001, http://app.internet.gov.sg/scripts/mfa/pr/read_content.asp?View,1119.

and strategic interests in two particular areas. These are: (1) preventing the emergence of exclusionary trade blocs; and (2) ensuring that the major economic and political players of the world stay engaged and focused on East and Southeast Asia, a region which is crucial to its own stability and prosperity.

Ample evidence of this thinking emerges from a review of Singapore foreign policy during the past few years. During this period, the credibility of existing regional institutions came under a good deal of criticism, mainly because of their handling of the 1997 economic downturn. But instead of withdrawing from them, Singapore has searched for ways to reform existing institutions, and where possible, create new ones to supplement them. This is reflected in its continued engagement in regional bodies such as ASEAN, APEC and ARF (and now ASEAN Plus Three). It is also seen in its support for the Asia-Europe Meeting (ASEM) process, and its proposal to create the Forum for East Asia-Latin America Cooperation (FEALAC).

The year 2001 was not a particularly creative year for ASEAN. The divisive intra-mural debate over ASEAN's non-interference principle appeared to have subsided.[23] Thailand, which had called on ASEAN to address the domestic problems of members that have regional implications, took a more traditional line on sovereignty under a new government. This was in line with Singapore's own approach. There were no major new initiatives, save for the special Declaration on Joint Action to Counter Terrorism, issued at the 7th ASEAN Summit held in November in Brunei. It promised measures such as intelligence-sharing, sharing best practices of national law enforcement agencies, and conducting training in the investigation and monitoring of terrorist acts.[24] Overall, the grouping struggled to dispel lingering questions about its continued relevance and effectiveness. Contributing to this climate of uncertainty were the renewed regional economic crisis, doubts about the member states'

---

[23] Amitav Acharya, *Constructing a Security Community in Southeast Asia: ASEAN and the Problem of Regional Order*, London and New York, Routledge, 2001.
[24] ASEAN, "2001 ASEAN Declaration on Joint Action to Counter Terrorism", Bandar Seri Begawan, Brunei, November 5, 2001, http://www.aseansec.org.

commitment to the ASEAN Free Trade Area (AFTA), disillusionment on the part of new members over limited gains from joining ASEAN, the absence of Indonesian leadership, lingering intra-mural tensions between key members such as Singapore and Malaysia and Thailand and Myanmar (although tensions on both fronts eased later in the year), and persisting international criticism of ASEAN's admission of Myanmar. Most observers agreed on the need for the grouping to "reinvent" itself. But the terms of reform remained a matter of debate, especially when they concerned the pace of institutionalization and the issue of sovereignty.

APEC's prospects seemed more discouraging than ASEAN's. In a normal year, the October 2001 APEC summit in Shanghai, the first to be hosted by China during a year in which Beijing gained admission into the WTO, would have carried much symbolic importance. But this symbolism was lost amidst the global turmoil and regional downturn. The summit might be remembered for two reasons. The first was the issuance of the 12-year-old grouping's first political statement, which strongly condemned terrorism, and the decision of host Jiang Zemin to conduct the entire proceedings in English. On economic matters, the summit expressed "full confidence in the medium and long-term growth prospects for the Asia-Pacific" on the grounds that the economic fundamentals of member states remained "sound". But little concrete action was proposed, beyond the enunciation of a "pathfinder approach" that would allow its more advanced economies to take the lead in advancing new initiatives for trade and investment liberalization.[25] While taking a useful declaratory stand against terrorism, APEC did not seem to have the mandate or capacity to undertake more concrete action in combating this evil, against which the primacy of the UN framework was officially acknowledged at Shanghai.

The ASEAN Regional Forum (ARF) had no chance to debate the terrorist issue, having held its annual ministerial session on July 25, 2001. Its main concern for the year was the operationalization of

---

[25] *The Straits Times*, October 22, 2001.

preventive diplomacy (PD), the second of the three-stage agenda
outlined in the 1995 Concept Paper which has served as a roadmap
for the grouping (the other two stages being confidence-building
and conflict resolution). Here, progress has been painfully slow, primarily owing to disagreements about sovereignty and non-interference. China views PD as a potential instrument for interference in
its internal affairs and seeks to exclude intra-state conflicts from its
scope. Against this backdrop, the adoption of three papers at the
Hanoi ARF meeting was encouraging. The papers dealt with the
concept and principles of preventive diplomacy, enhancement of
the role of the ARF Chair, and creation of a register of eminent persons who could be called upon to make recommendations to the
ARF on regional security matters requiring collective action.

Despite skepticism over its accomplishments to date, the ARF
remains the "most important venue" for discussion of security issues,
as the Chinese Foreign Minister Tang Jiaxuan put it. Singapore
offered a realistic assessment of the ARF at Hanoi. The ARF, in the
words of Foreign Minister S. Jayakumar, "helps to cushion tensions
and manage difficulties. It might not be able to solve disputes or prevent the outbreak of conflicts, but it can minimize their impact".[26]
This observation might be comforting enough for those who believe
in the usefulness of multilateral security approaches, for in a coun-
terfactual way, it suggests that without the existence of regional
groups like ASEAN and the ARF, tensions between the US and
China or intra-ASEAN conflicts linked to the Asian economic crisis
might have been even worse. It would be hard to prove this point,
but neither can it be dismissed as empty rhetoric coming as it did
from the foreign minister of a nation known for its reliance on balance of power approaches.

During the year 2001, the momentum in regional institution-
building clearly belonged to the ASEAN Plus Three process. The
origins of this idea could be traced to Malaysia's proposal for an
East Asian Economic Grouping (EAEG, later renamed as a Caucus,
or EAEC) in 1990 to counter the threat of regional trade blocs in

---

[26] *The Straits Times,* July 26, 2001.

Europe and the Americas. The EAEC had remained dormant during the first half of the 1990s owing to strong US opposition and limited enthusiasm on the part of Japan. Like Tokyo, Singapore had been reluctant to endorse a forum that would alienate and exclude the US. It had instead pushed for the institutionalization of APEC, making a successful bid to host its secretariat in Singapore. But the APEC process suffered from Japan's opposition to the US trade liberalization agenda and Malaysia's continuing disdain for Australia's active role in the forum. The outbreak of the Asian economic crisis saw APEC, lacking any mechanism for financial cooperation and sidelined by the role of global financial institutions like the IMF, lose considerable ground. Its championing of unfettered globalization and open regionalism was discredited. The ASEAN Plus Three process was the major beneficiary of this, its appeal enhanced by Japan's push for regional monetary cooperation (despite strong US objections) and China's emergence as an economic powerhouse that could become a regional engine of growth. The practice of East Asian leaders meeting jointly with their EU counterparts under ASEM had already created a precedent for ASEAN Plus Three. The latter was initiated by ASEAN in Manila in 1999 as an important part of its attempt to expand its reach and regain momentum.

The ASEAN Plus Three Summit held on November 24, 2001 in Brunei was notable for the assurance by China that ASEAN faced no economic threat from China's rapid economic growth and entry into the WTO. It even proposed a China-ASEAN Free Trade Area. At the summit, Prime Minister Goh highlighted the two "big ideas" to emerge from the deliberations: an East Asia Free Trade Zone and an institutional link between ASEAN and Northeast Asia. A study group formed to examine the prospects for both is due to report within a year on whether and how to institutionalize ASEAN Plus Three. But while Singapore sees the nascent forum as a useful vehicle for engaging Northeast Asia, it takes a cautious line on institutionalization. As Mr Goh put it at the outset, "I see no problem in ASEAN Plus Three evolving...into some kind of East Asia summit. But there are implications. I myself would not recommend a hasty evolution. We need the United States to be in East Asia. This is not an attempt to shut out Washington from Asia".[27]

The latter point reaffirmed the twin premises of Singapore's global and regional engagement: to keep the major powers, especially the US, focused on East Asia,[28] and to prevent the emergence of discriminatory regional blocs in the global economy. While Singapore has championed regionalism, it has consistently sought to keep it "open" and outward-looking, embedded firmly within larger global cooperative frameworks. This is reflected in Singapore's strong support for two inter-regional forums. The first is the Asia-Europe Meeting (ASEM), whose main institutional body, the Asia-Europe Foundation, is located in Singapore. The other is the Forum for East Asia-Latin America Cooperation (FEALAC), the idea for which originated from Goh Chok Tong himself in 1998. These two groups reflect Singapore's efforts to develop ties that bind the major growth regions of the world economy: East Asia, Europe, Latin America and North America.

Asian concerns that ASEM receives only limited attention from European leaders appear to be confirmed by the release in 2001 of a European Commission Strategy paper. In clear indication of how poorly ASEM's importance to the quest for an East Asian regional identity is understood in Europe, the paper called for bringing Australia and New Zealand into ASEM. While ASEAN and the ARF were reaffirmed as the "major focus" of the EU's political and security dialogue with Southeast Asia, the paper called for a separate process of building an "enhanced partnership" with China (a "regional power" which is becoming a "major competitor to developed economies in the region and beyond", and whose "increasing economic power is likely to translate into growing...assertiveness on the regional and international scene") and India (whose "role as a regional and global player merits special attention", and which is a

---

[27] Carlyle A. Thayer, "ASEAN Ten Plus Three: An Evolving East Asian Community?" *Comparative Connections*, 4th Quarter, 2000.

[28] Singapore failed to secure India's admission to ASEAN Plus Three, but India was accepted for a separate summit with ASEAN in the same overall annual gathering.

non-member of ASEM). The European Commission's indication that human rights, good governance and transparency would be placed at the center of political dialogues with ASEAN implied further hindrances to the development of ASEM. Chris Patten, the EU's commissioner for external relations, stressed that the admission of Myanmar had already diminished ASEAN's standing in the EU.[29]

If Singapore had hoped that ASEM might lead to increased trade and investment between the two regions, this has not materialized as yet. EU investment in Asia, although not insubstantial, has actually declined in recent years. Pascal Lamy, the EU's Trade Commissioner, suggests that this has as much to do with the Asian economic crisis as to the lack of a transparent and non-discriminatory investment regime in Asia. A disappointing ASEM gathering in Seoul in October 2001 prompted questions about the relevance of the five-year-old process. Singapore sees ASEM's problems as having much to do with a lack of "mutual respect". Ambassador-at-Large Tommy Koh, the former Executive Director of the Asia-Europe Foundation (ASEF), laments that "most Europeans still do not regard Asians as their equals".[30] Yet, he insists that ASEM remains important to Singapore for economic, political and even cultural reasons. The ASEM process helps to offset American political and cultural dominance. Also, by providing East Asian nations with an opportunity to collectively engage the EU, it ensures that East Asia "can constitute a pole in a multipolar world".[31]

Unlike ASEM, FEALAC was built upon meager economic foundations. In 1999, only 6 percent of Latin America's exports headed for Asia, while the former was the destination of 2.5 percent of Asia's exports. But during a visit to Latin America in June 1999, Prime Minister Goh was impressed by the dramatic pace of economic change in Latin America and "alarmed" by the fact that East Asians did not quite understand the phenomenon. The emergence of

---

[29] *The Business Times*, November 6, 2001.
[30] *The Straits Times*, May 14, 2001.
[31] Tommy Koh, "East Asia and Europe have an Important Date", *International Herald Tribune*, October 19, 2001.

regional blocs in Latin America, such as Mercosur, the Rio Group and the Free Trade Area of the Americas raised the prospect that Latin America was poised for a dramatic take-off at Asia's expense ("this place will take off like a bullet while Asia is going to be left behind").[32] FEALAC, as the "missing link" in Singapore's inter-regional strategy, could serve a two-fold purpose: to seek new trading and investment partners for Asia at a time of economic downturn in Asia itself, and to offer an avenue for engaging the US so as to limit the protectionist turn of Latin American free trade regimes. The FEALAC initiative offers further evidence of Singapore's strategy of using regional and inter-regional links to carve out greater economic and political space for itself in an increasingly competitive global economy.

While inter-regionalism is one pillar of Singapore's defense of openness in the global economy, the other is its pursuit of bilateral trade arrangements. Singapore has signed Free Trade Agreements (FTAs) with New Zealand and Japan, while negotiations are ongoing with the US, Australia and Mexico (other potential partners are Canada and the European Union). Malaysia sees Singapore's bilateral initiatives as a threat to ASEAN's own trade liberalization agenda, creating a "trojan horse" or "backdoor" through which outside countries can enter the AFTA. Singapore officials have been at pains to refute such criticisms, insisting that its bilateral FTAs complement AFTA and act as building blocks for global trade liberalization. They comply with AFTA's rules of origin as well as WTO rules. Singapore is merely "ahead of the curve" in pursuing trade liberalization on multiple fronts.[33] Once their benefits are demonstrated, the FTAs would create healthy pressure on other ASEAN members to accelerate their own liberalization through a similar mix of instruments. A case in point is Thailand, which has endorsed Singapore's FTA approach and has itself explored similar FTAs with other countries. Describing as a "non-issue" the controversy over the FTAs,

---

[32] *The Straits Times*, April 4, 2001.

[33] Ramkishen S. Rajan, Rahul Sen and Reza Siregar, *Singapore and the New Regionalism: Bilateral Economic Relations with Japan and the US* (February 2001), cited in *The Business Times*, April 25, 2001.

Heng Swee Keat, the CEO of the Trade Development Board, argued, "Singapore's FTA efforts can provide the catalyst to bring about the closer integration of ASEAN with our major trading partner economies in Asia, Europe and Americas. This will in the long-run bring strategic benefits for ASEAN. We must bear in mind the rise of regionalism globally". An FTA with the US, in his view, would be a "positive sign signaling US interest in ASEAN".[34]

Conclusion

In hard times, Singapore's foreign policy has reaffirmed its fundamentals. In the war against terrorism, it sided squarely with the US while stepping up homeland security to reduce its own vulnerability to terrorist attacks. In the economic arena, Singapore offered a clear affirmation of its commitment to the global economy, by forging bilateral and inter-regional linkages that would engage the world's major economic powers.

The basic framework for Singapore's response to the twin challenges of terrorism and protectionism has already been established. But the challenges could worsen in the years to come. A prolonged and largely unilateral American war against terrorism could create fresh political dilemmas for Singapore at home and within the region. In that event, foreign policy will have an important role in developing domestic understanding and regional consensus against terrorism. A single-minded pursuit of bilateralism, unless backed by greater neighborly consultations and consensus, would implicate Singapore further as a self-seeking unilateralist. Dealing with these challenges will pose a hard test of Singapore's ability to reconcile pragmatism with principle, and interest with engagement.

---

[34] Interview with Heng Swee Keat, CEO of Trade Development Board, *The Business Times*, June 13, 2001.

4

Waging the War on Terror: Singapore's Responses and Dilemmas[1]

Introduction

The war on terror, launched and spearheaded by the United States in response to the catastrophic attacks on the World Trade Center and the Pentagon on September 11, 2001, has presented the international community with difficult choices. On the one hand, the threat posed by terrorism to world peace and stability is universally recognized, especially by those states which themselves are facing this menace. In the aftermath of the September 11 attacks, the US drew worldwide sympathy and promises of cooperation from nations across continents and civilizations in its quest to punish the perpetrators. On the other hand, the international community remains sharply polarized over aspects of the war on terror waged by the Bush administration. Three elements of the US response have proven to be especially divisive. The first is the Bush administration's penchant for unilateral action. The second is the Bush doctrine of

---

[1] This chapter was originally presented as a paper at the Singapore Perspectives 2004 Conference, organized by the Institute of Policy Studies, Singapore, January 13, 2004 and appears as a chapter in Arun Mahizhnan, ed., *Singapore Perspectives 2004: At the Dawn of a New Era*, Singapore, Marshall Cavendish Academic and Institute of Policy Studies, 2004.

preemption. The third is the attack on Iraq, which the Bush administration initially justified by citing Iraq's alleged possession of weapons of mass destruction — a justification which has not been backed by credible evidence even after the US victory in Iraq.

Despite its overarching nomenclature, there is no single "war on terror". The latter is a continuing multidimensional and multifront effort; some aspects of which enjoy greater legitimacy in the international community than others. In the past year, Singapore has been involved in two important facets of the war on terror. The first is its efforts to disrupt and destroy the Jemaah Islamiyah (JI) network and protect Singapore from potential terrorist attacks. The second is its response to US expectations for support from its allies for the war to effect regime change in Iraq, a war which Washington has presented to the international community as an integral part of its war on terror. While the first challenge was operationally more demanding, the second has proved to be politically challenging.

Singapore's Anti-terror Efforts

Although terrorism had been recognized as a danger to Singapore before the September 11 attacks, there was clearly no sense of its magnitude prior to the attacks. As Prime Minister Goh Chok Tong put it, "We knew that it could be a problem, but we did not know the size of it. We knew there that there were local organizations which were prepared to use terror against the governments, but we thought they were regional, local. We did not know they were tied up with al-Qaeda".[2] The arrest of 31 men since late 2001 believed to be JI members seeking to bomb the US embassy and other foreign missions as well as local targets put Singapore on the global map of terrorist targets. The Bali bombings in October 2002 heightened the sense of vulnerability to the JI terrorist network. The foiled JI plan to bomb targets in Singapore was seen as a major relief; had it been

---

[2] *Online Newshour*, May 7, 2003, http://www.pbs.org/newshour/bb/asia/jan-june03/goh_05-07-03.html.

carried out, it could have been one of the deadliest terrorist attacks in the world since September 11. Referring to the fact that the arrested suspects were attempting to buy some 17 tons of ammonium nitrate to make seven huge truck bombs, a Singapore government report noted: "if carried out, [the plot] would certainly have caused loss of lives, physical injury, and ... considering the huge amount of ammonium nitrate which they intended to acquire, the consequences would have been catastrophic".

The arrests did not, however, lead Singapore to let its guard down against the threat posed by terrorism. The year 2003 saw a further intensification of Singapore's counterterrorism drive. In February 2003, Tony Tan, the Defense Minister (and later Coordinating Minister of Security), urged Singaporeans to be "psychologically prepared" for a terrorist attack.[3] He pointed to Singapore's "high visibility as a target" for groups like al-Qaeda and JI.[4] True, Singapore had foiled a significant terrorist plot at home. "But", as Prime Minister Goh Chok Tong warned in May 2003, "terrorism is an ongoing thing and unless it is eradicated in Southeast Asia and in the Middle East and other parts of the world, we, being a very open country which has taken action on terrorism, must expect ourselves to be vulnerable — to be a target in the future".[5] Goh even implied that Singapore might have become a higher-priority target for terrorists than its neighbors. As he put it, "the Bali bombing came about because they were actually targeting Singapore". Terrorists had "discovered that Singapore had become a hard target because our people were on the alert, all the prized targets were heavily, shall we say, guarded by our security authority; then they decided they must somehow explode a bomb somewhere, and they chose a soft target in Bali. It's unfortunate for Indonesia, but the lesson was, and still is, we have to be on guard against the terrorists". His joint statement with President Bush during

---

[3] *Agence France Presse*, "Singapore Ups Spending for Defence, Homeland Security", Singapore, February 28, 2003, http://www.singapore-window.org/sw03/030228a1.htm.

[4] *Agence France-Presse*, "Singapore: Support for US Makes it Top Terror Target", May 24, 2003.

[5] *Online Newshour, op. cit.*

the latter's visit to Singapore in October 2003 recognized that, while "much headway had been made in disrupting terrorist networks...more needed to be done and that the campaign against terrorism required a sustained long-term effort".[6]

What has been this "sustained long-term effort"? Singapore's overall response to terrorism may be divided into three areas: homeland security, bilateral cooperation and multilateral measures.

Homeland security

At the national level, Singapore has developed a framework of homeland security with a view to ensure greater inter-ministerial coordination, improve sharing of intelligence, and enhance its capacity for joint action involving civilian and military forces in countering terrorism. Unlike the US, where the Department of Homeland Security resulted from the merger of numerous government agencies, Singapore has adopted a network approach comprising several inter-ministerial agencies: the National Security Task Force and the Homefront Security Center under the Ministry of Home Affairs, the National Security Secretariat under the Ministry of Defense, and the Joint Counter Terrorism Center, which coordinates intelligence on terrorists. In 2003, Singapore increased its spending on homeland security by 13.6 percent to $2.31 billion from $2.04 billion.[7] Among the steps undertaken as part of Singapore's homeland security policy are:

- The establishment of a special committee to oversee airport security, after a JI member was said to be planning to hijack a commercial jet and crash it into Singapore's international airport.
- "Hardening" of key infrastructure and installations like Jurong Island, with its many petrochemical companies, against terrorist

---

[6] *USA Today*, "Bush Talks Terror with Singapore Leaders", October 21, 2003, http://www.usatoday.com/news/world/2003-10-21-bush-asia_x.htm.

[7] *Agence France Presse*, "Singapore Ups Spending for Defence, Homeland Security", *op. cit.*

attacks. New security measures include increased police patrols on potential targets, soldiers reinforcing security at military and selected civilian installations.

- Intensified security measures to protect more public areas, such as Holland Village and Boat Quay, including restrictions on vehicle parking and increased security patrols.
- Strengthened border controls, including full checks on all vehicles, passengers and baggage at land border checkpoints with Malaysia.
- Exercising contingency plans for scenarios such as major fires and bomb explosions.
- Security briefings for target audiences such as security managers of commercial buildings, owners of entertainment outlets and grassroots organizations in order to create security awareness, educate the target audience of the need for security and how they can play a role in prevention and response.
- The creation of Community, Safety and Security Programs (CSSP) for the general public which bring together residents, grassroots leaders and neighborhood police officers to identify the safety and security concerns of the neighborhood precinct and mobilize other residents and relevant partners to help address these problems.
- Deployment of air marshals on Singapore Airlines flights in an effort to forestall possible hijackings and terror attacks.

Bilateral cooperation

At the bilateral level, Singapore's main partner in the war on terror has been the United States. In September 2002, Singapore became the first port in Asia to participate in the Container Security Initiative, which allows US inspectors to check cargo bound for US destinations for possible shipments of explosives or weapons of mass destruction. Another key area of US-Singapore counterterrorism is intelligence-sharing. In an interview with the American *Newshour* program, PM Goh Chok Tong alluded to this aspect of US-Singapore relations: "Where the information concerns Singapore, we do receive information from the FBI which, of course, enables us to take steps to prevent acts being committed against us".[8]

A major milestone in US-Singapore security ties is the decision to work towards a Framework Agreement for the Promotion of a Strategic Cooperation Partnership in Defense and Security. This was announced on October 21, 2003 by President Bush and Prime Minister Goh Chok Tong during the former's visit to Singapore. The Bush visit, in the words of a joint statement, reflected "the strong and multifaceted US-Singapore partnership, which saw the signing of the US-Singapore Free Trade Agreement earlier this year, and on a history of cooperation, congruent interests, and shared perspectives". The proposed Framework Agreement, to be concluded "as soon as possible", would expand bilateral cooperation in counterterrorism, counterproliferation of weapons of mass destruction, joint military exercises and training, policy dialogues and defense technology.[9]

It is noteworthy that despite deepening security ties, Singapore has not sought the "major non-NATO ally" status that Thailand and the Philippines currently enjoy with the US. This conforms to historical circumstances — Singapore was not part of the original postwar San Fransisco Treaty system, unlike Manila and Bangkok — and possibly to a realization that such a designation might be a needless provocation to terrorist groups and some of its neighbors already wary of the Republic's close defense links with the US.

Singapore's security cooperation with its immediate neighbors, Malaysia and Indonesia, is affected by recent problems in bilateral ties. But bilateral tensions have not precluded intelligence-sharing against terrorist groups. According to PM Goh Chok Tong, Singapore enjoys "very good cooperation from both Malaysia and Indonesia. The intelligence authorities do meet and they do exchange notes". While Singapore was critical of Indonesia's earlier reluctance to acknowledge the problem of terrorism and take firm action against terrorist groups, it now endorses Jakarta's post-Bali counterterror initiatives: "Because of the Bali bombing, the [Indonesian] government has moved to arrest

---

[8] *Online Newshour, op. cit.*

[9] U.S. Department of State, http://usinfo.state.gov/topical/pol/terror/texts/03102107.htm.

several key people. Still, quite a few are on the run, but the main thing is both Indonesia and Malaysia and Singapore are cooperating to exchange information on their whereabouts and to apprehend them".[10]

Multilateral and regional measures against terrorism

On the multilateral front, Singapore is a party to the ASEAN-United States of America Joint Declaration for Cooperation to Combat International Terrorism,[11] a document signed on August 1, 2002, with a view to create "a framework for cooperation to prevent, disrupt and combat international terrorism through the exchange and flow of information, intelligence and capacity-building".[12] At the regional level, Singapore works within the framework of ASEAN, the ASEAN Regional Forum and the Asia-Pacific Economic Cooperation (APEC) to combat terrorism. Some of the initiatives undertaken by these organizations include:

- Promoting common adherence to international conventions on terrorism to integrate them with ASEAN mechanisms;

---

[10] *Online Newshour, op. cit.*

[11] ASEAN, "2001 ASEAN Declaration on Joint Action to Counter Terrorism", Bandar Seri Begawan, Brunei, November 5, 2001, http://www.aseansec.org.

[12] The agreement seeks to:

- Continue and improve intelligence and terrorist financing information-sharing on counterterrorism measures, including the development of more effective counterterrorism policies and legal, regulatory and administrative counterterrorism regimes.
- Enhance liaison relationships amongst their law enforcement agencies to engender practical counterterrorism regimes.
- Strengthen capacity-building efforts through training and education; consultations between officials, analysts and field operators; and seminars, conferences and joint operations as appropriate.
- Provide assistance on transportation, border and immigration control challenges, including document and identity fraud to effectively stem the flow of terrorist-related material, money and people.

- Calling for the early signing/ratification of or accession to all relevant anti-terrorist conventions including the International Convention for the Suppression of the Financing of Terrorism;
- Designating Principal Contact Points in all ASEAN member countries on counterterrorism matters along the lines of Singapore's Joint Counter Terrorism Center (JCTC);
- Holding meetings of ASEAN police chiefs to discuss practical measures and explore avenues of cooperation against terrorism;
- Increasing cooperation among front-line law enforcement agencies in combating terrorism and sharing "best practices";
- Providing for greater exchange of information/intelligence on terrorists and terrorist organizations, their movement and funding, and other information needed to protect lives, property and the security of all modes of travel;
- Strengthening existing cooperation and coordination between various ASEAN agencies to counter terrorist organizations, their support infrastructure and funding and bringing the perpetrators to justice;
- Developing regional capacity-building programs to enhance existing capabilities of ASEAN member countries to investigate, detect, monitor and report on terrorist acts;
- Sharing technical expertise and best practices through training workshops;
- The ARF Agreement on Measures Against Terrorist Financing.

While terrorism has come to occupy the center-stage in ASEAN and regional organizations and interactions involving ASEAN and outside powers, a good deal of it consists of declarations and statements of intent, which are not necessarily backed by concrete measures. In most cases, such cooperation amounts to exchanges of information and intelligence, sharing of best practices and capacity-building programs, rather than joint planning and operations against terrorist groups. The year 2003 saw ASEAN and the EU issuing a Joint Declaration on Cooperation to Combat Terrorism at the end of the 14th ASEAN-EU Ministerial Meeting in Brussels on

January 28, 2003, which "reiterated the commitment of the two sides to work together and contribute to the global efforts to stamp out terrorism".[13] Another development was the ARF Statement on Cooperative Counter-Terrorist Actions on Border Security dated March 22, 2003, geared to development of cooperative measures to strengthen security at their borders against terrorist threats. The ARF also convened its first inter-sessional meeting on counterterrorism and transnational crimes (ISM-CT/TC), cochaired by Malaysia and the US, in Sabah in March 2003, which resulted in a call for increased cooperation in intelligence-sharing as well as in enforcement measures against terrorist threats.[14] A potentially more substantive development was an agreement among ASEAN police and law enforcement officials calling on each ASEAN member state to establish an antiterrorism task force to strengthen cooperation on counterterrorism and to collaborate with the affected ASEAN member country following a terrorist attack. The type of assistance that could be requested could include identifying, pursuing and apprehending suspects, examination of witness(es), searching and seizing evidence, evacuating and treating of victims, forensic and crime laboratory analysis.[15]

Regional cooperation on counterterrorism remains constrained by divergent national priorities, lingering bilateral disputes and unequal national security capabilities. Singapore sees regional cooperation as a complement to national and bilateral efforts, rather than a substitute. While the common fear of terrorism has created a new sense of purpose in ASEAN, the political cohesion of the group remains shaky over the other aspect of the global war on terror that took center-stage in 2003: the US invasion of Iraq.

---

[13] ASEAN, "ASEAN Efforts to Counter Terrorism", http://www.aseansec.org/14396.htm.

[14] ASEAN, "Report of the ARF Inter-sessional Meeting on Counter-Terrorism and Transnational Crime", Karambunai, Sabah, Malaysia, March 21–22, 2003, http://www.aseansec.org/15133.htm.

[15] ASEAN, "ASEAN Efforts to Counter Terrorism", *op. cit.*

The War Over Iraq

Responding to the threat posed by terrorist groups such as JI and al-Qaeda creates its own political dilemmas for Singapore, which has to bear in mind the potential repercussions of counterterrorism on its own Muslim population. But the most controversial development in the war on terror during the past year has been the US invasion of Iraq. The forced regime change in Iraq is particularly damaging to world order because the most principled criticisms of the US action come from America's allies in the developed West, rather than its usual detractors in the Third World. The belated US justification of the war as a humanitarian effort to rid Iraqi people of a murderous regime has not been convincing, given that the war was initially presented as a counter to Iraq's alleged possession of weapons of mass destruction (WMD).

In contrast to Europe, where the war created a major split within NATO, America's allies in Asia have generally closed ranks with the US. Expediency and pragmatism, stemming from security dependence on the US in the face of continuing geopolitical threats and a traditional faith in the US-led regional balance of power order, have outweighed considerations of principles at stake in the weakening of the multilateral order. All the treaty allies of the US, Japan, South Korea, Philippines and Thailand found reasons of "national interest" to back the US attack on Iraq. Singapore, though not a party to the San Fransisco system of alliances, has followed the same course, basing its decision on the exigencies of its national interest.

A clear sense of Singapore's position on Iraq came from Foreign Minister S. Jayakumar a week before the actual start of combat operations. In remarks to the Parliament on March 14, the Minister indicated that Singapore's stance on Iraq would be guided by the issue of Iraqi compliance with UN Security Council resolutions calling for its immediate disarmament. It was "imperative that Iraq disarm immediately and comply with all United Nations Security Council Resolutions"; hence, if there was to be "a use of force, it must be because of Iraq's failure to comply". The Minister argued that this was not a "new position", but dated back "many years to the Gulf War when we joined the international community then in condemning Iraq's aggression against Kuwait as totally unacceptable under international law and the UN Charter".

The minister described "the danger of WMD falling into the hands of terrorists, terrorist organizations or extremist groups" as not a "hypothetical risk":

> Iraq's possession of illegal WMD is, post 9/11, an unacceptable threat. If Iraq gets away without disarming, it will send a very bad signal to extremist groups across the world. The fact that the Security Council cannot reach consensus on a second resolution cannot be taken as an excuse for inaction... it is in our fundamental national interest to see Iraq disarmed. This is necessary to send the right signal to extremists and other states like North Korea that are trying to develop WMD, as well as to non-state players like terrorists and extremist groups whose threat to the world will be enhanced if they get their hands on WMDs.

On the question of whether Singapore was being too pro-US, he responded, "We are not pro-US; we are not anti-any country. Then what are we? We are being **pro-Singapore**". While Singapore "strongly advocate[s] US's continued presence and engagement in this region" and has "excellent bilateral relations with the US... that does not mean that we are subservient to the US or that we agree with everything that the US does, or says, or requests, without regard to our own national interests".[16]

The US launched its invasion of Iraq on Thursday, March 20, 2003. Two days later, Deputy Prime Minister Tony Tan presented the first official position of the Singapore government on the attack by pledging to allow the US the use of Singapore's military facilities during the campaign: "We will allow US aircraft to fly over Singapore ... allow US military assets and ships and aircraft to call at Singapore to use our military bases. We have made these facilities available to the US during this

---

[16] S. Jayakumar, Remarks in Parliament on "Strategic Review in the World, Including the Situation in Iraq, and Asia-Pacific Region", March 14, 2003, http://www.mfa.gov.sg/iraq.html#Iraq.

campaign as we did in the campaign in Afghanistan". Singapore allowed itself to be named as a member of the "coalition of the willing". Later, after the US victory in Iraq, Singapore would dispatch 192 Singapore Armed Forces (SAF) personnel to provide logistics support for the Iraqi reconstruction, even as it remained mindful of the international controversies surrounding the justification of the war and the consequences of the anti-US backlash for its security.

Singapore's leaders invoked national interest as the main justification for the Republic's support for the US invasion of Iraq. On March 20, 2003, DPM Tony Tan stated, "We must make our decisions on what is in the best interest for Singapore and there has been no monetary and other inducements paid to Singapore by the US to support the US position".[17] Comparing Singapore's support for the war with the opposition expressed by the leaders of Malaysia and Indonesia, PM Goh noted, "But we take different positions out of our own national interest, out of our own calculations regarding the future of our own security".[18]

A more specific justification was voiced by the Minister for Trade and Industry George Yeo during a trip to the US to promote the bilateral free trade agreement. According to Yeo, "Singapore supported the US on Iraq because it recognized that US leadership is indispensable in the world today, especially in the war against global terrorism. If Saddam Hussein could thumb his nose at the US, other rogue governments and organizations would have been encouraged to create mischief as well".[19] This seemed to stress the need to protect US credibility, rather than implying concurrence with the Bush administration's stated justifications for the attack, which centered on weapons of mass destruction.

---

[17] While Singapore neither received nor needed the kind of financial inducements from America that might have lured others into the "coalition of the willing", the fact that the war came at a critical final stage of negotiations of the US-Singapore free trade agreement was not lost on observers.

[18] *The Straits Times*, "Moderate Muslims Know Goal in Iraq: PM Goh", March 29, 2003.

[19] George Yeo, Speech at the US Chamber of Commerce, April 28, 2003, http://app10.internet.gov.sg/scripts/mfa/pr/admin/ussfta_list_title_SGdisplay.asp? View,15.

Goh Chok Tong himself stressed the dangers posed by Iraq's attempt to acquire weapons of mass destruction as the basis for Singapore's support for regime change in Iraq. During a trip to Japan, Goh stated, "It is clear to everyone, unless that person wears blinkers, that this is a war to remove the weapons of mass destruction from Saddam Hussein".[20] Singapore had to support the US because "If weapons of mass destruction were to fall into the hands of terrorists, they could also become a threat to Singapore, which two years ago was targeted by a terrorist group".[21]

What Goh did not specify, of course, was whether in Singapore's view, Saddam was in actual possession of such weapons. This made his stance different from Tony Blair, who had insisted on intelligence information pointing to Iraqi possession of such weapons which could be deployed at very short notice. Goh's invoking of the weapons of mass destruction was to stress the strategic rationale for the war, at a time when the war was being perceived by sections of the Muslim population as being an anti-Islam crusade. Indeed, Goh presented Singapore's support for the war in the context of its wider security concerns and interests. Hence, his assertion that the war was about getting rid of Iraq's weapons of mass destruction was apparently designed to underscore the point before Singapore's Muslim population that this "is not an Islamic issue, or a case of the West trying to hit out at Islam".[22]

While Singapore is a significant beneficiary of its cooperation with the US in coping with transnational terror, the war on terror is not without costs for Singapore's security and political interests, costs which are not lost to the government. One such cost has to do with the spill-over effect of the growing anti-Americanism in Singapore's neighborhood. Tony Tan acknowledged this when he

---

[20] *The Straits Times*, "Moderate Muslims Know Goal in Iraq", *op. cit.*

[21] *Ibid.*

[22] *Ibid.* Subsequently, as the failure of occupying US forces to find any credible evidence of an active Iraqi program to acquire weapons of mass destruction fuelled an international controversy over the war's purpose, the Foreign Ministry reacted strongly to a commentary in the *Straits Times* questioning the government's support

warned on January 4, 2004 that Singapore is a prize target for terrorists because of its support for the US war on terror.[23]

A second cost was alluded to by PM Goh in his speech to the Asia
Society on May 7, 2003, when he acknowledged that "the Iraq War
catalysed opposition to US pre-eminence ... the resistance of France,
Russia, Germany and others in the UN Security Council's reaction
against Iraq has raised grave questions about the future of the UN".[24]
Considering that the UN has been recognized by Singapore's foreign
policy-makers as a bulwark of the sovereignty of small states, a significant weakening of this institution cannot but be detrimental to the
Republic's strategic interests. This realization informs Singapore's
desire to see an enhanced UN role in the rebuilding of Iraq, a desire
expressed by Goh during his meeting with Japanese Prime Minister
Junichiro Koizumi.[25] Yet, given the current political climate in US-
UN relations, this remains unfulfilled.

The divisive effect of the war on international order and the dangers posed by rising anti-Americanism to the interests of America's

---

for the US. On June 11, Foreign Ministry spokeswoman Tan Lian Choo said in a letter
to the newspaper that the search for the weapons was "still ongoing and nobody at
this point in time can say conclusively that there was no WMD in Iraq." Singapore was
"not embarrassed" by the US failure to find WMD so far, and had taken a "strong, principled and consistent position on Iraq based on Singapore's national interests." Tan
concluded by saying that Singaporeans "cannot afford to strike postures fashionable
with the oppositionist media in America and Britain at the expense of the security of
Singaporeans" and that "a small nation in terrorist-infested Southeast Asia does not
have this luxury of libertarian posturing." See Tan Lian Choo, "Singapore's Support
for Action on Iraq Prompted by Wider Concerns", *The Straits Times*, Forum Pages,
June 11, 2003. See also *Agence France Presse*, "Singapore Defends Support for War on
Iraq, Says Weapons Search Not Over", June 11, 2003. The article to which she was
responding appeared on June 7, 2003 in *The Straits Times* as "No Sign of Iraqi Weapons:
How Now, Singapore?", by Tan Tarn How, a columnist with the paper.

[23] *The Straits Times*, "S'pore Lays Out Plans to Beat Airline Terrorists", January 4, 2004,
http://straitstimes.asia1.com.sg/topstories/story/0,4386,228460-073339940,00.html.

[24] Goh Chok Tong, Speech at Asia Society, May 7, 2003, http://www.asiasociety.org/
speeches/tong03.html.

[25] *Asian Political News*, "Koizumi, Goh Agree on U.N. Role in Postwar Iraq", March 31,
2003, http://www.findarticles.com/cf_dls/m0WDQ/2003_March_31/99448274/
p1/article.jhtml.

allies were clearly articulated by Senior Minister Lee Kuan Yew. Speaking at the 2nd Shangri-La Dialogue in May 2003, Lee noted:

> Throughout history, every force has generated a counter-force. For the present, Russia, China and many countries in the European Union want to maintain good or friendly relations with the United States. There is reason to hope that tending to these relations can prolong US pre-eminence. Not to do so may persuade more nations that the way to restrain American unilateralism is to join a group of all those opposed to it.[26]

Lee's advice to the US against unilateralism was grounded not on idealist principles of international conduct (which has been blamed for the current US-European divide by Robert Kagan in his juxtaposition between European Kantianism and American Hobbesianism). Rather, it derived from the core assumptions of realism, which believes in the tendency of absolute power to invite countervailing responses from rival powers and coalitions. While other Southeast Asians, such as Prime Minister Mahathir of Malaysia, had criticized the US for neglecting the root causes of terror and doing little to address the unjust suffering of the Palestinians, Lee's comment, coming from a long-standing ally of America with a reputation for clear-eyed *realpolitik*, was perhaps a more telling warning against the long-term dangers posed by American unilateralism that might damage the interests not just of the hegemon itself, but also that of its allies like Singapore.

---

[26] Lee Kuan Yew, "After Iraq", Address to the 2nd Shangri-La Dialogue, May 30–June 1, 2003, http://www.iiss.org/shangri-la-more.php?itemID=10.

5

Singapore and Southeast Asia in a Fast-changing Landscape: Coping with the Rise of China and India[1]

Facing the Rise of China and India

For the past several years, few foreign policy issues have attracted more attention and statements from Singapore's leaders than the rise of China and India and its impact on the regional security landscape. "China and India will shake the world", is how Minister Mentor Lee Kuan Yew put it when he addressed the inaugural conference of the LKY School of Public Policy titled, "Managing Globalization: Lessons from China and India".[2] Senior Minister Goh Chok Tong asserted, "The rise of China and India will shift the global economic centre of gravity from West to East".[3] Prime Minister Lee Hsien Loong told the ASEAN Business and Investment Forum:

---

[1] This paper was originally prepared for the Singapore Perspectives 2006 Conference on "Going Glocal: Being Singaporean in a Globalized World", held at the Island Ballroom, Shangri-La Hotel, January 12, 2006. I would like to thank Manisha Cheong, a research intern at IDSS during December 2005, for providing valuable research assistance in preparing this paper.

[2] Lee Kuan Yew, Address to the LKY School of Public Policy, April 4, 2005.

[3] Goh Chok Tong, Speech at the Nomura Singapore Seminar, November 8, 2005.

The rise of China and India is transforming the entire region. China has already overtaken the US as the major trading partner of many Asian countries, including Japan, Korea and several ASEAN economies. India opened up several decades after China — the initial pace of reform was slow, but India has made significant progress in recent years. Combined, these two economic powerhouses will shift the centre of gravity of the world economy towards Asia.[4]

Foreign Minister George Yeo remarked to the Chinese language paper *Lianhe Zaobao*:

So there's China, there's India, then we see, what about ourselves? Where do we stand in the face of all this? Will we be left behind? ... the rise of China and India has galvanised us both as individual economies and collectively as a region.[5]

The need to help fashion a new regional security architecture in response to the rise of China and India has become one of the priority areas of Singapore's foreign policy. Its response has two aspects. One aspect is informed by a traditional balance of power thinking, which involves, among other things, developing closer security ties with the US and other regional players, including India. On the other hand, Singapore has pursued a regionalist approach, by pushing for greater ASEAN economic integration and supporting a broader East Asian Summit with the participation of India as well as Australia and New Zealand. The need for a "collective response" to the rise of China and India has also provided an additional imperative for mending fences with its more immediate neighbors, Indonesia and Malaysia, with whom Singapore's relations had suffered a major reversal since the outbreak of the Asian economic crisis in 1997.

---

[4] Lee Hsien Loong, Address at the 3rd Asean Business and Investment Forum, December 11, 2005.

[5] George Yeo, Interview, *Lianhe Zaobao*, October 7, 2005.

The Balance of Power Imperative

Commenting on Singapore's foreign policy, the late Michael Leifer observed: "Singapore's leaders have consistently approached the matter of foreign policy from the conventional realist perspective of a small state obliged to cope with a world that was potentially hostile and without common government".[6] Lee Kuan Yew, who continues to be an authoritative voice on Singapore's foreign policy, also remains the most articulate exponent of the city-state's "realist" view of international relations, perhaps more so than the younger leaders of Singapore. Lee's worldview accords a central place to the balance of power, although as this paper will argue later, he tends to use the term "balance" quite liberally but hardly literally, thus allowing room for differing interpretations and misinterpretation by observers. As one of the first statesmen in the world to recognize the wider geopolitical impact of China's phenomenal economic growth in the 1980s, last year he restated a message which has been well-recognized by the city-state's foreign policy elite for over a decade: "There is no question that China will cause a major displacement in the balance of power when she finally arrives as a major player on the world scene, say 30 years hence".[7] But what is relatively new is the recognition of India's potential to become a major Asian and global economic and strategic actor, and its impact in reshaping the regional geopolitical landscape. Lee characteristically views the implications for India's rise in balance of power terms; thus, Singapore wanted India in the East Asian Summit because it "would be a useful balance to China's heft".[8] Also, he sees the US military presence in Singapore and Asia "as a stabilising and benign" factor which will help "balance the growing weight of China".[9]

---

[6] Michael Leifer, *Singapore's Foreign Policy: Coping with Vulnerability*, London, Routledge, 2000, p. 98.

[7] Lee Kuan Yew, Interview with Arnuad de Borchgrave, Text at http://app.mfa.gov.sg/.

[8] Lee Kuan Yew, "Lee Kuan Yew Reflects", *Time Asia*, December 5, 2005, http://www.time.com/time/asia/covers/501051212/lky_intvu.html.

[9] Lee Kuan Yew, Interview with de Borchgrave, *op. cit.*

It is clear that the balancing act in Singapore's foreign and security policy is directed at China, rather than India. China is, and will likely remain for some time, a security concern for Singapore. Singapore, which is not a party to the territorial dispute in the South China Sea, does not see China as a direct military threat to its sovereignty and territorial integrity. But it worries about Chinese bullying and the "volatility" of its domestic politics, which, driven by nationalism, could translate into belligerent behavior towards neighbors like Singapore.[10] India on the other hand is seen as part of Singapore's balancing options vis-à-vis China in which relations with the US remains central.

A state balances its rivals in two ways (not mutually exclusive): internally by building up its national military and economic strength, and externally by developing alliances with major powers. Singapore, for whom no amount of national self-strengthening would suffice against China, has looked predictably to the US for external support. To be sure, Singapore sees its strategic relations with the US in a broader context of its national security concerns, which includes perceived threats from its immediate neighbors. The US presence also acts as a force for stability which in Singapore's view at least has facilitated regional economic growth. But the China factor is undoubtedly one of the concerns driving the US-Singapore relationship. Singapore's strategic relations with the US moved closer in 2005 when in July, the two countries signed a "Strategic Framework Agreement for a Closer Cooperation Partnership in Defense and Security".[11] Conceived during a 2003

---

[10] Thus, referring to the Chinese reaction against Lee Hsien Loong's visit to Taiwan shortly before he took over as Prime Minister in 2004, Lee Kuan Yew commented: "The discomfort [with China] is primarily that it is becoming a very powerful country and that it's not averse to making its power felt. For instance, when we did not sufficiently make amends for having visited Taiwan, they just froze all economic ties at the official level. We are a very small part of their economy, but they are a significant part of ours — and they are fully aware of this. It's a lever they will use from time to time". Lee mused that "The day before yesterday, I was an old friend of China; today I'm a new enemy. It's volatile". Interview with *Time Asia*, *op. cit.*

[11] States News Service, White House Press Statement, Transcript, July 12, 2005.

meeting between President George W. Bush and then Prime Minister Goh Chok Tong, this agreement designates Singapore as a "Major Security Cooperation Partner". It builds upon the extensive range of security ties that the two countries have developed since Singapore's offer of military facilities to the US in 1990 to offset the loss of the latter's Philippine bases. This agreement had led, among other things, to the shifting of a regional headquarters for the US navy in Singapore, which in recent years has handled about 100 US ship visits annually.[12] After the 9/11 attacks, Singapore was prompt in participating in the US-sponsored Container Security Initiative (CSI), which permits US agents to "pre-inspect" shipments to the US, and Proliferation Security Initiative (PSI), which seeks to monitor and prevent transport of nuclear material which might be used for illegal purposes.[13] Both the initiatives had been developed by the Bush administration as part of the so-called "war on terror". Although nominally multilateral, they are largely dictated by US security concerns and policies, being more of the "coalition of the willing" variety. The Strategic Framework Agreement consolidates and advances bilateral defense ties, providing for an annual strategic dialogue, joint military exercises and training covering regional threats as well as peacekeeping missions, and expanding Singapore's access to US defense technology.[14] Two other agreements were signed during the Singapore Prime Minister's visit. Defense Minister Teo Chee Hean and Defense Secretary Donald Rumsfeld inked an agreement which, according to a Pentagon fact sheet, would "build on the extensive interactions" between the two armed forces "to further expand military cooperation, including developing military expertise and defense capabilities to deal with the wider range of non-conventional threats facing armed forces today".[15] Finally,

---

[12] Anthony L. Smith, *Special Assessment: The Asia-Pacific and the United States 2004–2005*, Honolulu, Asia-Pacific Center for Security Studies, 2005, p. 1.

[13] *Ibid.*, pp. 1, 4–5.

[14] States News Service, July 12, 2005; BBC Monitoring Service, July 13, 2005.

[15] *Inside the Pentagon*, July 14, 2005.

Singapore and the US also updated and extended the agreement over US access to military facilities in Singapore signed in 1990, which was due to expire in 2005.[16]

Bush described the Strategic Framework Agreement as moving the bilateral "relationship beyond the economic, to a strategic relationship", a misstatement of sorts, since fairly substantial strategic ties between the two already existed. Prime Minister Lee expressed appreciation for the "strong, consistent" stand of the US in combating terrorism globally. Yet, the telling aspect of the Agreement was the designation of Singapore as a "Major Security Cooperation Partner", rather than "major non-NATO ally", a status conferred on Thailand and Philippines, both of whom are treaty allies of the US from the Cold War days, in the wake of the US invasion of Iraq. This is entirely to the liking of Singapore. Minister Teo would describe US-Singapore ties as a "special relationship" binding two nations who are "more than just friends", but not allies. Singapore's reasons for not entering into a formal defense alliance with the US is intended to reduce provocation to Malaysia and Indonesia, which have, publicly at least, expressed discomfort and suspicion about the underlying motives behind the city-state's defense links with the US.

Moreover, Singapore's approach to China's power is not entirely identical with that of the US. Lee Kuan Yew has often questioned the wisdom of the US in adopting the more extreme version of the balance of power approach: containment, which sections of the US policy-making elite have advocated and will continue to advocate. For Lee, a containment policy will heighten Chinese insecurity and trigger a nationalist backlash that would destabilize the Southeast Asian security environment.[17] Lee Kuan Yew is not hopeful that the "line drawn [by the US] across the Taiwan Straits can be held for very long".[18] In the event of the Sino-US war over the Taiwan Straits

---

[16] BBC Monitoring Service, July 13, 2005.

[17] Amitav Acharya, "ASEAN and Conditional Engagement", in James Shinn, ed., *Weaving the Net: Conditional Engagement with China*, New York, Council on Foreign Relations, 1996, pp. 220–248.

[18] Lee Kuan Yew, Interview with de Borchgrave, *op. cit.*

that might prompt a US request to use its Singapore facilities, Singapore will face a dire dilemma, similar to Australia's, which has indicated that its support for the US in such a war cannot be automatically assumed. Despite having a closer understanding with the US, compared to Indonesia and Malaysia, on the threat posed by terrorism, Singapore also remains wary of aspects of the US war on terror, especially the invasion of Iraq based partly on this rationale. Despite having supported the US invasion formally, Singapore's policy-makers now realize that the war in Iraq might have a negative impact on its security environment, especially if local extremists develop links with the terrorist organizations fighting the US occupation of Iraq.

If one constraint on Singapore's balance of power approach was indicated in the designation of the US-Singapore relationship, another came from departing US ambassador Frank Lavin. Ambassador Lavin chose his farewell dinner speech in October to warn that "Singapore will pay an increasing price for not allowing the full participation of its citizens". Singapore had "proud" achievements and the US would "stand side-by-side with Singapore", because, in Lavin's *bushspeak*, "My view of foreign policy is simple: We — America and Singapore — are the good guys". But the US ambassador also wondered: "in this era of web logs and webcams, how much sense does it make to limit political expressions?"[19]

These words were picked up in far away Washington, where the conservative *Washington Times* covered it under the title "Embassy Row".[20] Ambassador Chan Heng Chee deftly nipped any controversy in the bud by describing Lavin "as a friend of Singapore's" who "knows Singapore will change".[21] But the episode served as a reminder that unlike Australia and the US, Singapore and the US are not "natural allies", even if both are "the good guys". It is unlikely that the US will make the political differences an obstacle to the bilateral strategic and economic relationship, as long as Singapore supports its war on terror, and as long as Washington sees the need for a

---

[19] James Morrison, "Embassy Row", *The Washington Times*, October 13, 2005.
[20] *Ibid.*
[21] *Ibid.*

military presence in Singapore to respond to the rise of China and support its deployments to the oil-rich Persian Gulf through Southeast Asia's strategic sea lanes. But it also means the US-Singapore relationship, a cornerstone of Singapore's balance of power approach, will be driven mainly by economic and strategic imperatives. Depending on how far "Singapore will change" its domestic system, the relationship may remain subject to their differing values and lack the "we feeling" required for the development of a true and long-term security community.

Functionalism and Economic Interdependence

The balance of power metaphor so often applied to describe Singapore's foreign policy towards China and India belies a much more eclectic, complex and diverse strategy adopted by its policymakers. Diplomatic accommodation, economic interdependence, and regional cooperation and socialization play a major role in the way Singapore has responded to the rise of China and India.

The first visit by the new Singapore Prime Minister to China happened in October 2005. It was especially significant because of the row between the two countries over Lee Hsien Loong's unofficial visit to Taiwan in July 2004. The Chinese reaction then was swift and vigorous: "Whatever pretext the Singaporean leader uses for his visit to Taiwan", the Chinese Foreign Affairs spokesperson had insisted, "the visit will damage China's core interest and the political foundation for China-Japan relations".[22] Beijing's retaliation included a freezing of official economic exchanges. Singapore defended Lee's visit as an unofficial event before he assumed the Prime Minister's job, aimed at learning more about the domestic situation in Taiwan that would have enormous implications for Singapore and the region. But it was also quick to reaffirm the One China policy, not

---

[22] Qiyue Zhang, Statement on Singaporean Deputy Prime Minister Lee Hsien Loong's Visit to Taiwan, July 11, 2004, http://www.chinaembasseycanada.org/eng/xwfw/ 2510/2535/t142801.htm.

only for itself, but also for the whole of Asia. "If Taiwan goes independent", said Lee Hsien Loong on August 12, 2004, "Singapore will not recognize it. In fact no Asian country will recognize it". This act of accommodation drew a favorable response from Beijing; it "accords well with the interest of Singapore", said the Chinese Foreign Ministry.[23]

Lee Hsien Loong's October 2005 visit resulted, in his own words, in "a good series of meetings" with Chinese leaders held in a "strategic and regional context", which showed a "convergence of views".[24] Chinese leader Hu Jintao accepted Lee's invitation to visit Singapore. But the idea of a bilateral Singapore-China Free Trade Agreement wanted by Singapore is still held back by Beijing, which has concerns about its impact on China's overall regional trade liberalization strategy. This not withstanding, Foreign Minister George Yeo would later describe the outlook for Singapore-China relations as "very bright".[25] Singapore's dealings with China were aimed not only at developing a good understanding between their two countries, it was also Singapore's policy to "help China establish enduring good relations" with all the ASEAN members.[26]

Singapore's diplomatic relations with India has required no fence-mending. The end of the Cambodia conflict had removed the key barrier to the political relationship between India and ASEAN that had emerged over India's recognition of the Vietnamese-installed Heng Samarin regime in Cambodia, which ASEAN had fought to deny international legitimacy. But India and Singapore have to go much further to bring their economic relationship closer to the level now obtaining between Singapore and China. Bilateral Singapore-China trade amounted to S$60 billion in 2005.[27] By comparison, Singapore-India trade was $11.5 billion in 2004.[28] This has much to do

[23] *China Daily*, August 25, 2005.
[24] *The Business Times*, October 27, 2005.
[25] BBC Monitoring Service Asia-Pacific, December 30, 2005.
[26] *Xinhua News Agency*, December 30, 2005.
[27] *Ibid.*
[28] *Reuters News*, April 25, 2005.

with the fact that India's economic reforms were at least two decades behind that of China. Nevertheless, Singapore's economic links with India are accelerating; although the estimate by the Association of Chambers of Commerce and Industry of India, a national business network, that trade between the two countries could reach US$50 billion by 2010 is perhaps too optimistic.[29] Singapore's investments in India, although small compared to its investments in China, are increasing rapidly. The city-state, according to one report, was the third largest foreign investor in India overall.[30] And links are flourishing in other areas, such as tourism traffic. There are 117 weekly passenger flights between India and Singapore covering 10 Indian cities.[31] Some 1,500 Indian companies have set up a presence in Singapore, with over 300 Indian information technology firms maintaining software development centers in the city-state.[32]

A further boost to Singapore-India economic ties was given during Lee Hsien Loong's visit to India in June to sign the Comprehensive Economic Cooperation Agreement (CECA). The agreement, covering tariff reduction and elimination provisions, tax benefits for Singapore companies in India and investment promotion, would, hoped Indian Prime Minister Manmohan Singh, be a "historic" deal that would pave the way for a "quantum jump" in trade and investment flows.[33] During Lee's visit, Singapore and India also signed agreements on mutual legal assistance and prevention of terrorist money laundering. Singh described Singapore as India's gateway to Southeast Asia.[34]

While Singapore's economic links with India lags with that of China, its defense links with India are substantially closer. Defense and security cooperation was discussed during Teo Chee Hean's visit to China in November, representing the first visit by a Singapore

---

[29] *Indian Business Insight*, June 30, 2005.

[30] *Agence France Presse*, August 25, 2005.

[31] *Ibid.*

[32] *Indian Business Insight*, June 30, 2005.

[33] BBC Monitoring Service Asia-Pacific, June 30, 2005.

[34] Channel News Asia, June 29, 2005.

Defense Minister to the country since 1997.[35] During the visit, the two sides announced steps to hold an annual defense policy dialogue, increase cooperation over international humanitarian assistance and provide scholarships for members of the People's Liberation Army to study in Singapore. But these pale in significance in relation to the defense links that have emerged between India and Singapore. The two countries already have a Defense Cooperation Agreement. In 2005, their naval exercises were upgraded with the holding of a new series, called Singapore-India Maritime Exercise. Whereas the previous naval exercises (code-named *Lion King*) between the two countries, started in 1994, were held annually off Indian waters, this new exercise was conducted in the South China Sea. The choice of South China Sea was "not a signal to be given to somebody", said the commanding officer of the Indian Navy's Eastern Fleet in an obvious reference to China. Instead, "We are showing our presence here so that Indian ships, ships flying the Indian flag, have a feeling of security".[36] But apart from the location, the nature of these exercises was suggestive; it was not about anti-terrorism, but included anti-piracy and anti-submarine operations as well as maritime interdiction. Moreover, in January, Singapore and India signed a Memorandum of Understanding to hold their first ever joint army exercise, which was held a month later in areas near Delhi and Mumbai. This came after the first bilateral air exercise between the two countries was held in 2004.[37]

Singapore's day-to-day relations as well as long-term agreements with China and India are conducted primarily at the bilateral level. But bilateralism has its limits, as evident in the row over Lee Hsien Loong's visit to Taiwan. Hence, multilateral relations offer an additional margin of comfort and safety for Singapore from big power whims and intransigence. At the core of Singapore's multilateral approach to cope with the rise of China and India was deepening

---

[35] *The Straits Times*, November 17, 2005.
[36] *The Hindu*, March 6, 2005.
[37] *The Hindu*, January 19, 2005.

ASEAN cooperation through legalization and institutionalization and expanding the scope of the fledgling East Asian cooperation.

Restoring Good Neighborliness

But none of these approaches would go very far if Singapore's relations with its immediate neighbors, Indonesia and Malaysia, remained mired in disputes and suspicions. Although Singapore's relations with its immediate neighbors are important in their own right, they also have significant impact on overall regional cooperation. For example, few things have damaged the credibility of ASEAN more in the wake of the 1997 regional economic crisis than the bickering and bad blood between Singapore and Malaysia and Singapore and Indonesia over the question of aid and related issues.

Singapore's bilateral relations with Indonesia and Malaysia went through a bout of fence-mending in 2005. Many factors contributed to this: restored confidence in Malaysia and to a lesser extent Indonesia over their respective economies; and change of leadership in all the three countries, especially the transition from Mahathir to Abdullah Badawi in Malaysia and the advent of a more stable leadership in Indonesia. But one other contributing factor was Singapore's realization that in dealing with the regional behemoths, China and India, economic and diplomatic bilateralism or power-balancing with US support (in relation to China) would not suffice. Regional solidarity and integration was also an essential part of the response. This collective response required not only overcoming strained intra-mural relations within ASEAN, but also the growing institutionalization and integration of ASEAN and the development of an open and inclusive East Asian regionalism.

The improvement of Singapore's ties with Indonesia was more pronounced. Lee Hsien Loong and Susilo Bambang Yudhoyono had already held four bilateral meetings before the East Asian summit in December, including a symbolically important retreat in Bali immediately after the 2nd terrorist attacks in October. Among the items on the agenda included were a Defense Cooperation

Agreement, a Counterterrorism Agreement, as well as the more contentious matter of an extradition treaty.[38] Indonesia's request to have such a treaty to deal with the outflow of illegal funds by corrupt officials and business people from Indonesia has been resisted by Singapore, which insists that it already has adequate laws to deal with financial crimes. But the economic relationship between the two countries has improved. Singapore was among the top five investors in Indonesia between 2001 and 2004.[39] Between January to June alone, Singapore was in effect the biggest investor in Indonesia with 108 approved projects totaling US$591 million.[40] On the defense front, the two countries launched a joint surveillance system to exchange information about shipping instantaneously in the Singapore Strait to augment the Indo-Singaporean Coordinated Patrols (ISCP).[41] Furthermore, Singapore's armed forces played an important role in bringing aid to tsunami-hit Aceh, which helped to lift considerably the city-state's sometimes dismal image in Indonesian society.[42]

But perhaps the most notable improvement in Singapore-Indonesia relations concerned not the substance, but the style of negotiations, with the two sides agreeing not to conduct bilateral relations by "megaphone diplomacy" through public statements and the media when "negotiations on sensitive issues and future cooperation are ongoing".[43] There is an element of irony here — one of the worst instances of bilateral megaphone diplomacy was President Jusuf Habibie's hurtful naming of Singapore as a "little red dot", precisely the title of a collection of reflections and remembrances by Singapore's diplomats published in 2005.[44]

---

[38] *The Straits Times*, October 18, 2005.

[39] *Agence France Presse*, October 17, 2005.

[40] *The New Paper*, July 15, 2005.

[41] *The Straits Times*, May 18, 2005.

[42] *Agence France Presse*, October 17, 2005.

[43] George Yeo, in Parliament, cited in *The Straits Times*, October 18, 2005.

[44] Tommy Koh and Chang Li Lin, eds., *The Little Red Dot: Reflections by Singapore's Diplomats*, Singapore, World Scientific, 2005.

The outlook for Singapore's relations with Malaysia was less rosy, but nonetheless marked by some bright spots. The overall tone of bilateral relations was a major shift from the Mahathir days. Malaysia remained Singapore's top trading partner with S$88.3 billion total trade in 2004.[45] The megaphone diplomacy between the two countries was down, if not entirely out. Under Prime Minister Badawi, Malaysia had called for a "pluck the low-hanging fruits first" approach to bilateral relations. The benefits of this approach was indicated in April, when the two countries signed an agreement to mark the "full and final settlement" of their dispute over Singapore's land reclamation work at Tuas and Palau Tekong in the Johor Straits. In September 2003, Malaysia had taken Singapore to the International Tribunal for the Law of the Sea over the issue, complaining about its adverse impact on navigation, the local environment and livelihood of Malaysian fishermen caused by the reclamation. The court had ruled in Singapore's favor to continue its reclamation work. Under the deal, Singapore could continue its reclamation, but agreed to pay S$300,000 for maintenance works at a Malaysian jetty, adjust its reclamation plans to protect sea currents and pay S$98,550 to compensate Malaysian fishermen for the loss of income. The "civil and civilised manner" in which the reclamation issue was settled, stated George Yeo, "gives us confidence that our bilateral disputes can be settled in the same way" through third party adjudication of arbitration and "on the basis of mutual benefit and mutual respect".[46] His Malaysian counterpart, Syed Hamid Albar, described the deal as a "milestone in Malaysia-Singapore relations", which "shows very clearly that our collaboration over more than a year to bring a satisfactory conclusion to an issue of great importance to our two countries" and that "there is nothing impossible if we put our hearts and minds together to find a resolution".[47] He also noted that Malaysia and Singapore had referred their dispute over Pedra Branca to the International Court of Justice and both have agreed to be bound by whatever judgment the court would pass.[48]

---

[45] *Agence France Presse*, August 19, 2005.

[46] Channel News Asia, April 26, 2005; Reuters News, April 26, 2005.

[47] Channel News Asia, April 26, 2005.

[48] *Ibid.*

Whether this is wishful thinking and whether the "hearts and minds" of the two nations can really come together will be tested in the coming years, as the two countries deal with several other outstanding disputes, including the "Crooked Bridge" or "Convoluted Half-Bridge" issue (Malaysia's plan to go ahead with its own half of a proposed bridge to replace the existing Johor-Woodlands causeway if Singapore maintains its opposition to the bridge idea), the supply of Malaysian water to Singapore at prices acceptable to both sides, and the issues of Malayan Railways Land in Singapore, the ban on Singapore military over flights in Malaysian airspace and pension contributions by Malaysians working in Singapore.

The bilateral issues dividing Singapore, Malaysia and Indonesia did not prevent cooperation over maritime security issues. The three countries now conduct Coordinated Patrols (as opposed to more integrated Joint Patrols) in the Malacca Straits to counter piracy, armed robbery and terrorism. These patrols were augmented by an "eye-in-the-sky" maritime air surveillance system to provide intelligence. In December, the three sides announced plans for a set of standard operating procedures that would allow hot pursuit of offenders to each other's territorial waters.[49]

The Multilateral Imperative: Ideas, Identity and Institution-Building

Singapore has sometimes been portrayed as a reluctant regionalist *vis-à-vis* the balance of power approach to regional order, or less of a believer in the ASEAN idea and regional identity than as a selective utility-minded partner in functional regional cooperation. The utilitarian attitude remains. As George Yeo would put it, the members of ASEAN "are being driven together, not so much by a natural affection for one another as by huge challenges which confront us collectively".[50]

---

[49] BBC Monitoring Service, December 11, 2005.
[50] George Yeo, Address at the Global Leadership Forum in Kuala Lumpur, September 6, 2005, http://www.mfa.gov.sg/internet/.

No analysis of Singapore's foreign policy has paid attention to the importance of regional identity and community, and the same can be said of much of the academic work on ASEAN.[51] Yet, these have become an increasingly important part of the discourse on regionalism in Southeast Asia and East Asia. Reflecting this trend were a series of statements by Singapore's leaders on the importance of the ASEAN idea, and the need for ASEAN to develop a collective identity through greater popular interest and participation in regional projects.

As Foreign Minister, George Yeo set the tone by acknowledging the importance of the ASEAN idea and the historical sense of regional identity which underpins ASEAN regionalism:

> ...there is a coherence in Southeast Asia which we know exists and grows stronger by the day. Some historians explain that, whatever our diversity, we are still a collection of states which lie along the trade routes between East Asia and South Asia, alternately receiving the cultural influence of both, and, more recently, from the West. Because Southeast Asia was never united as one political entity, there is tolerance for diversity, a willingness to syncretize, a cosmopolitan spirit which welcomes foreigners in our midst and the mixing of blood, especially among members of the elite.[52]

Why this talk about regional identity (i.e., "coherence in Southeast Asia") now? One reason, as could be seen from the context of Yeo's remarks, was the need to fashion a regionalist approach to the rise of China and India which is in tune with the historical memory and experience. This was not about recovering the past, but a sense that

---

[51] Only a handful of studies on ASEAN had dealt with regional ideas, identity and important variables in regional cooperation and foreshadowed the current debates about ASEAN's direction, such as the ASEAN Security Community and the issue of regional identity. See Amitav Acharya, *The Quest for Identity: International Relations of Southeast Asia*, Singapore, Oxford University Press, 2000; Acharya, *Constructing a Security Community in Southeast Asia: ASEAN and the Problem of Regional Order*, London and New York, Routledge, 2001; Jurgen Haacke, *ASEAN's Diplomatic and Security Culture*, London, RoutledgeCurzon, 2002.

[52] George Yeo, Address at the Global Leadership Forum, *op. cit.*

the past can be a guide to the future in developing Singapore's regional environment in which China and India are once again the two dominant elements. Thus:

> Every time the east-west trade flourished, we prospered with it. The growth of the east-west trade in this century will dwarf anything that has ever been seen before and will open up a whole new horizon for us.

The strategy that might result from this historical context could be thus outlined:

> ...in every area, we have to think and act strategically so that Southeast Asia becomes a major intermediary between China and India. This is our historical position and this should also be our future.[53]

But making Southeast Asia a major intermediary between China and India requires cohesive regionalism backed by stronger institutions. A key element of this strategy is the proposed ASEAN Charter. The goal of the ASEAN Charter is to create an international legal personality for ASEAN. ASEAN began life with a Declaration (the Bangkok Declaration) rather than a Charter, and has hitherto avoided legalistic and formal approaches to cooperation. Singapore, which had been lukewarm to the earlier Indonesian proposal for an ASEAN Security Community, especially the idea of a regional peace-keeping force, has embraced the idea of an ASEAN Charter more enthusiastically. Singapore's Prime Minister Lee Hsien Loong described the objective of the ASEAN Charter as being to "set a clear and ambitious long-term direction for ASEAN".[54] George Yeo explained that the Charter was necessary because it would make ASEAN "integrated and economically vibrant" and create "effective

---

[53] *Ibid.*

[54] Amitav Acharya, "Challenges for an Asean Charter", *The Straits Times*, October 24, 2005.

institutions" to face the rise of China and India. Although he doubted "if ASEAN integration will ever reach even half the level of integration in Europe today", there was "no other road ... Either we become stronger as a region or we will fragment".[55]

While ASEAN is developing a legalistic charter that goes beyond the traditional ASEAN way of soft institutionalism, the issues of the "ASEAN Idea" and forging an ASEAN regional identity through socialization have also come into focus. "ASEAN's Quest for an Identity Gains Urgency", was the headline of a story appearing in the *Straits Times* on December 5. This and related stories reported the results of a survey among 1,000 English-speaking urban residents in Indonesia, Malaysia, Singapore, Philippines, Thailand and Vietnam on, among other things, whether "people in ASEAN identified with one another".[56] Although the survey also found doubts and skepticism about the pace of regional integration in ASEAN, it also revealed that six out of ten polled agreed that "people in ASEAN identified with one another". What is really important about this survey is not the numbers who did not agree with the question, but the numbers who did. The findings contradict the line of those, such as the late Michael Leifer, who have either ignored or dismissed "identity" (as well as ideas and norms) as a factor in ASEAN regionalism.[57] Only four out of ten Singaporeans made the same response, suggesting not only that "Singaporeans are laggards when it comes to willingness to integrate",[58] but also that Singaporeans are the least believers in a regional identity for ASEAN. This is hardly surprising, given the global orientation of Singapore's foreign policy and the latent skepticism in the Singaporean public about the merits of integrating with neighbors that can hardly match the city-state's economic and educational achievements or strong domestic institutions.

---

[55] George Yeo, Address at the Global Leadership Forum, *op. cit.*

[56] *The Straits Times*, December 5, 2005.

[57] For a discussion of Leifer's views and the identity debate, see Amitav Acharya, "Do Norms and Identity Matter? Community and Power in Southeast Asia's Regional Order", *Pacific Review*, vol. 18, no. 1, March 2005, pp. 95–118.

[58] *The Straits Times*, December 5, 2005.

Despite, or perhaps because of this factor, which could become a real obstacle to regional cooperation, Singapore's leaders have increasingly, and to some extent uncharacteristically, embraced ASEAN's growing "quest for an identity", which, incidentally, was almost identical to the title of this author's 2000 book, *The Quest for Identity*.[59] Hence, George Yeo, perhaps acknowledging that ASEAN's ability to offer a collective response to the changing strategic and economic environment required the inculcation among the Singaporean public of a sense of ASEAN identity, spoke of the importance of spreading "the ASEAN idea to all our people especially to the young, so that we internalize a greater sense of ASEAN citizenship".[60] Incidentally, 2005 was the first year in which the members of ASEAN celebrated the ASEAN Day: on August 8. Commenting on this development as a first step towards an ASEAN identity, Prime Minister Lee Hsien Loong urged that "For our citizens to identify with a broader ASEAN identity, this identity must be real and relevant. We need to find ways to promote among the peoples of ASEAN a deeper sense of belonging and community, and greater awareness of their common destiny … The fate of ASEAN ultimately lies in their hands".[61]

Stressing the social and ideational conditions for ASEAN's success may surprise those who believe that Singapore's foreign policy is too "realist" to find space for ideational variables. Yet, unless one characterizes statements by Singapore's foreign policy-makers about the regional idea and identity as "cheap talk" and allowing for some

---

[59] Acharya, *The Quest for Identity, op. cit.* The book argues that ASEAN's approach to regional order can be viewed as a "quest for identity", not in the sense that such an identity has already emerged or can be assumed, but that ASEAN regionalism is driven in no small measure by a regionalist imagination and an effort to develop a common identity out of considerable cultural, political and ethno-religious diversity. The main argument of the book is that ideas and identity matter in international relations of Southeast Asia, which cannot be explained by material forces and utilitarian calculations alone.

[60] George Yeo, Address at the Global Leadership Forum, *op. cit.*

[61] Lee Hsien Loong, Address at Asean 100 Leadership Forum, September 28, 2005, http://www.mfa.gov.sg/internet/.

inevitable gap between rhetoric and reality that can be found in the foreign policy of all nations, there is good reason to rethink the traditional understanding of Singapore's foreign policy as a relentless pursuit of military and economic instruments and hard utilitarian bargaining. The analysis of Singapore's foreign policy seriously engages an alternative explanation, which focuses on ideas, identity and socialization.

The idea of an East Asian Summit was not a Singaporean idea. Its ideational origins date back to Mahathir's proposal for an East Asian Economic Grouping (EAEG), later renamed as East Asian Economic Caucus (EAEC). Yet, the inaugural East Asian Summit in December 2005, which was to pave the way for an eventual East Asian Community, was closer to Singapore's conception of regional order than Mahathir's. This is because Singapore, along with Indonesia and Japan, had lobbied for the inclusion of India, Australia and New Zealand into the grouping. The rationale, at least from Singapore's point of view, was to counter possible Chinese dominance of the grouping or at least dilute its influence. This made the Summit appealing to Singapore, even though Mahathir himself would deride the event for including these non-East Asian actors.[62]

Some would describe Singapore's support for the broader East Asian summit as a classic balancing act by the city-state. This comes through clearly from a reading of Lee Kuan Yew's interview with *Time Asia*:

> It happened in an unplanned, almost accidental, way. Abdullah Badawi, the Prime Minister of Malaysia, offered to host an East Asia summit: ASEAN plus three — the three being China, Japan and South Korea. China's premier, Wen Jiabao, then offered to host the second summit. That would move the center of gravity away from Southeast to Northeast Asia and make some countries anxious. We agreed that we should also invite India, Australia and New Zealand and keep the center in ASEAN; also, India

---

[62] *Taipei Times*, "Mahathir Doesn't Want Australia at East Asia Summit", December 8, 2005, http://www.taipeitimes.com/News/world/archives/2005/12/08/2003283497.

would be a *useful balance* to China's heft. This is a getting-together of countries that believe their economic and cultural relations will grow over the years. And this will be a restoration of two ancient civilizations: China and India. With their revival, their influence will again spread into Southeast Asia. It would mean great prosperity for the region, but could also mean a tussle for power. Therefore, we think it best that from the beginning, we bring all the parties in together. It's not Asians versus whites. Everybody knows Australia and New Zealand are close to the US. There shouldn't be any concern that this is an anti-American grouping. It's a *neater balance.*[63] (emphasis added)

Mr Lee's use of the term "balance" ("useful balance" and "neater balance") needs closer scrutiny, because on the surface, it lends support to the realist view that Singapore's foreign policy is essentially about the balance of power. Yet, Lee uses the term to describe not the build-up of national military power and economic capacity and alliances with other powers against a rising China, but essentially a diplomatic maneuver: the act of bringing India, Australia and New Zealand into the East Asian multilateral grouping. This sort of a policy would be construed as balancing only if one interprets balance of power as a diplomatic move undertaken within the social context of regional institutions, where persuasion, rather than power politics, holds the centre-stage and where open and inclusive interactions trump unilateral or exclusionary measures in order to socialize a rising power which has the potential to threaten Singapore's and ASEAN's security. In other words, the meaning of "balance" here is institutional, rather than military. This may reflect the inherent ambiguities and multiple meanings of the term, but is hardly compatible with the conventional realist notion of power-balancing, no matter however qualified. If multilateral settings are so essential to the achievement of "useful balances" and "neater balances", then this is a huge concession to liberal and social constructivist approaches which challenge realism.

---

[63] Lee Kuan Yew, Interview with *Time Asia, op. cit.*

The development of East Asian cooperation faces numerous challenges, chief among these being the climate of mistrust and rivalry
between China and Japan, the lack of a concrete agenda of tasks,
duplication of functions with other regional institutions (APEC in
the economic realm and ARF in the security domain), and controversy and uncertainty over whether the summit, or the narrower East
Asian group called the ASEAN Plus Three (the ten ASEAN members
plus Japan, China and South Korea), will be the anchor for an eventual East Asian Community.[64] Singapore is likely to opt for the open,
inclusive and transparent formula of regionalism it has already
secured for the summit.

Conclusion: Survival Through Socialization

This leads to the conclusion of this essay: the foreign policy of
Singapore has not just been about ensuring survival through power-
balancing; it has also been about carving out a "regional existence"
(to use founding Foreign Minister S. Rajaratnam's words) through
socialization within regional institutions and processes. To understand and explain Singapore's foreign policy from a predominantly
"realist" or balance of power framework of international relations
would be simplistic. It would be to miss the much more complex setting within which the city-state now carries out its foreign policy initiatives. While Singapore might have indeed adopted a predominantly
realist worldview in the initial years of the Republic, when its survival
might have been really at stake, the city-state, like most nations of
the world, has had its own learning curve. While "survival" is a term
still employed by scholars and policy-makers to describe Singapore's
national interest, Singapore's foreign policy has increasingly recognized that long-term survival depends on securing acceptance as a
social and sociable member of the regional and international community.

---

[64] Amitav Acharya, "East Asian Integration is Test for Big Powers", *Financial Times*,
December 13, 2005.

Realism as a perspective on international relations sees the balance of power as the solution to the problem of ensuring international order.[65] Yet Singapore's foreign policy, including its response to the rise of India and China, features as much an effort to draw them into a regional system as balancing their power.

Realism also dismisses the role of ideas and identity in international relations. Yet, as Chan Heng Chee notes in her essay for the *Little Red Dot*, Singapore foreign policy-makers have recognized and made full use of the "power and possession of ideas, big ideas in international diplomacy", especially in developing regionalism.[66] Another key realist argument is that economic interdependence is a cause for conflict, rather than cooperation, in international relations. Yet, Singapore has consistently based its foreign policy and national security strategy on forging global and regional economic interdependence.[67] These tools have been used in coping with the rise of China and India, both bilaterally and multilaterally.

Realism, especially its more recent variant called neo-realism, sees international (including regional) cooperation as a fundamentally unattainable enterprise. Multilateral institutions matter only in the margins of international relations. Yet former Foreign Minister Wong Kan Seng lists "the fostering of ASEAN regional cooperation" as the second most important item in Singapore's "national interests", next only to the "protection of its sovereignty and independence" (the need to maintain a "stable balance of power in Southeast Asia" comes third).[68] Realists like Hans Morgenthau held that the concept of "national interest" is fundamentally defined in terms of the power variable. But as Wong suggests, the "national interest" can also be defined, or redefined as a state proceeds through incremental socialization

---

[65] Amitav Acharya, "Realism, Institutionalism and the Asian Economic Crisis", *Contemporary Southeast Asia*, vol. 21, no. 1, April 1999, pp. 1–29.

[66] Chan Heng Chee, "Friends and Ideas in Diplomacy", in Koh and Chang, eds., *The Little Red Dot*, pp. 111–116.

[67] See Chapter 2 of this book. See also Chan, *ibid.*

[68] Wong Kan Seng, "Continuity and Change in Singapore's Foreign Policy", in Koh and Chang, eds., *The Little Red Dot*, p. 50.

with other states, in terms of regional cooperation and institution-building. If foreign policy is basically about the pursuit of national interest, and if Wong can place ASEAN as the 2nd major element of Singapore's national interest, then this really should be indicative of the misleading nature of the almost exclusive emphasis that conventional accounts of Singapore's foreign policy have laid on the balance of power mechanism. In dealing with the rise of China and India, arguably the institutionalist strategy has as much a place as the traditional balancing mechanisms, such as closer defense ties with the US that are more of an insurance policy against potential Chinese hegemony, which even as hard-nosed Singaporean "realist" as Lee Kuan Yew does not take as inevitable.

Regional identification and interaction has been as much a tool for ensuring Singapore's survival and well-being as the balance of power approach, sparing it the fate of being the "Israel in Southeast Asia". Singapore policy-makers, perhaps more so among the new generation of leadership compared to the Lee Kuan Yew generation, have accepted and increasingly valued the regional idea and see in it a potent way for enhancing Singapore's interests. The conflation of national interest with the regionalist idea is least explained by realism; one needs to bring in other perspectives such as liberalism and social constructivism, which are much better able to deal with the pacific effects of economic interdependence and the role of ideas, identity and institution-building as tools for regional and international order.[69]

---

[69] Acharya, "Do Norms and Identity Matter?", *op. cit.*

APPENDIX

Statement of H. E. S. Rajaratnam, Minister for Foreign Affairs of Singapore, at the Opening Ceremony of the Inaugural Meeting of the Foreign Ministers of ASEAN, Bangkok, August 8, 1967

Mr. Chairman, Your Excellencies, Ladies and Gentlemen,

First of all, on behalf of my Delegation and the Government of Singapore, I would like to thank the Government of Thailand and its people for hosting this Conference of what is today, five countries and in the course of years to come of many more countries of South East Asia. Secondly, on behalf of my Delegation, I would like to extend particular thanks to our Chairman for the tactful, judicious and patient way in which he guided our not always coherent deliberations towards a more than successful conclusion. I would like to take this opportunity to thank the officers who did excellent work in translating our intentions into more concrete form by way of documents and papers.

So, today, after four days of rather pleasant and friendly discussions, we are about to launch the new ASEAN. It was easy to give birth to a new organization, but the creation of an organization of this nature is the most simple of all tasks. It is a mere skeleton that we have erected. Now the really difficult task is to give flesh and blood to this concept. We, in Singapore, are not unmindful of the fact that schemes for regional cooperation will run into more rocks than calm waters. Nevertheless, having had four or five days of discussions with my ministerial colleagues, there is one thing that is uppermost in my mind and that is the conviction of my ministerial colleagues in regard to both the inevitability and the desirability of regional cooperation. However, it would be necessary not only for ministers or leaders to take this new regional scheme seriously but also to transmit to its people the need for a new kind of thinking.

For twenty years each of us in this region had been compelled to do things purely on the basis of nationalist fervor. And many of us know that after twenty years of decolonization, nationalism alone has not provided or fulfilled the expectations by way of happier life, more fruitful life, better living standards to our countries and for our peoples. This realization has grown and, therefore, it is necessary for us if we are really to be successful in giving life to ASEAN to marry national thinking with regional thinking. We must now think at two levels. We must think not only of our national interests but posit them against regional interests: that is a new way of thinking about our problems. And that is two different things and sometimes they can conflict. Secondly, we must also accept the fact, if we are really serious about it, that regional existence means painful adjustments to those practices and thinking in our respective countries. We must make these painful and difficult adjustments. If we are not going to do that, then regionalism remains a Utopia.

The last point I would like to stress is that there may be, as has happened to other associations of this kind, misunderstandings as to what ASEAN is all about. So, I would like to stress that those who are outside the grouping should not regard this as a grouping against anything, against anybody. We have approached ASEAN as standing for something, not against anything. If there are people who misunderstand the proposed regional grouping, or manifest hostility towards it, let us explain that it can only be because as in Europe and in many parts of the world, outside powers have vested interests in the balkanization of this region. We ourselves have learnt the lessons and have decided that small nations are not going to be balkanized so that they can be manipulated, set against one another, kept perpetually weak, divided and ineffective by outside forces.

So, as far as we are concerned, we want to ensure a stable South East Asia, not a balkanized South East Asia. And those countries who are interested, genuinely interested, in the stability of South East Asia, the prosperity in South East Asia, and better economic and social conditions will welcome small countries getting together to pool their collective resources and their collective wisdom to contribute to the peace of the world. The more unstable South East Asia is, the more the peace of the world is also threatened.

So, I would urge people outside the region not to misunderstand this coming together of our five and other South East Asian countries. We want to ensure that ASEAN stands for the interests of ASEANs and therefore by implication for the peace and prosperity of the world. That is all we are interested in. And if other countries think of tomorrow and are willing to help us to achieve this objective, they will be welcomed as friends. And we will also be worthwhile friends to them.

However, in order to win over regard and respect from the outside world, we must first take ASEAN seriously ourselves. There are a lot of people watching what all this is going to amount to. So first we must take our own child seriously. We must convince those who are watching us that we are prepared to make the adjustments and sacrifices necessary to achieve our objective and we are serious about it. The message must get through that this time the South East Asian countries are not going to be like the Balkans during the last two World Wars; that they are not going to be pushed around; once other nations take us seriously, just as we take ourselves seriously; once there is acceptance of our role as a united grouping of Asian countries, then we can bring peace and prosperity to this region as well as to the rest of the world.

Address by S. Rajaratnam to the Singapore Press Club, February 6, 1972

Singapore: Global City

This is the text of an address to the Singapore Press Club on February 6, 1972 when S. Rajaratnam first used the term "global city" to describe the role and aspiration of Singapore and to explain the reasons for its economic success.

Source: Wee Teong Boon, ed., *The Future of Singapore — The Global City*, Singapore, Democratic Socialist Club, n.d., pp. 15–32.

What I propose to do is to elucidate an inexplicable mystery about Singapore — a mystery which some people find worrying and others somewhat irritating. And the mystery is this: Why has not an independent Singapore as yet collapsed? Worse still, why, instead of things getting progressively worse, are things getting better? Is all the progress and economic buoyancy in Singapore an illusion created by a cunning arrangement of mirrors? Or can the whole thing be attributed to good luck and happy accidents, such as the war in Vietnam and the political and economic difficulties of neighboring countries?

Some people appear to think so. That is why from time to time some commentators, including otherwise perceptive journalists, become anxious every time Singapore runs into an air-pocket. The higher Singapore flies, the greater, the fear is, will be the fall. Immediately after separation, the prognosis for Singapore was a gradual relapse into economic decay and mounting political turbulence.

When this did not happen, the fears gradually subsided.

Then came the announcement that the British were going to dismantle their bases and with it the substantial contributions they made to our economy. The general feeling was that this time Singapore would really get into trouble.

Again, the worst did not happen.

More recently, some of our neighbors, quite understandably, took measures to dispense with some facilities of Singapore's entrepot trade. Predictably, the professional mourners appeared proclaiming doomsday. True, our entrepot earnings dropped by 4.5 percent (or $30 million) in 1970. In fact, it has been dropping since 1960 when it constituted 19 percent of our Gross Domestic Product (GDP) to 11 percent in 1970. The indications are that our entrepot trade will continue to form a smaller and smaller percentage of our Gross National Product (GNP).

But despite the decline in our entrepot trade and the run-down of the British base, our GDP increased by 15 percent in 1970. Investments have flowed in, and unemployment, traditionally Singapore's sword of Damocles, instead of increasing, has decreased to the point that some sectors of our economy have to be manned by imported labor.

However, the jittery pessimist has not stopped biting his fingernails. As he sees it, facts and logic indicate that an independent Singapore cannot be viable. And let me say that the case against a viable independent Singapore is, at first sight, a formidable one.

As a matter of fact, my colleagues and I believed in it once — believed in it so strongly as to successfully bring about a merger between Singapore and Malaysia. I do not wish to spell out the case, as most of you are familiar with it. Briefly, it was that a small city-state, without a natural hinterland, without a large domestic market and no raw materials to speak of, had a near-zero chance of survival, politically, economically and militarily.

What then is wrong with the case against the survival of an independent Singapore? Where was the basic flaw?

One easy explanation offered is that we have thrived on happy accidents. For example, it is said that Singapore's prosperity is the consequence of the failure of our neighbors to realize their full economic potentialities. When they do, they will dispense with the services that Singapore has traditionally performed. Then, it will be curtains for Singapore.

My contention, which I shall elaborate later, is that the opposite is true. The more prosperous our neighbors become, the more dynamic their economies are, the greater will be the chances for Singapore's survival, and the better its economic prospects. Our economic relationship with them will of course be different. We cannot, as before, live by importing and re-exporting their raw materials. As I remarked earlier, the entrepot trade will constitute a declining percentage of our economy as our neighbors take over much of the trade themselves.

Nor can we, as we now do, live by selling them cheap textiles, shoes, slippers, chocolates and things like that.

The days for this kind of trading are numbered. We can no longer be the Change Alley of Southeast Asia, though in passing, let me say our Change Alley role is not something to be looked down upon. It not only helped to build the prosperity of Singapore, but it also contributed towards the economic development of Southeast Asia.

But times are changing and there will be less and less demand for the traditional type of entrepot services that Singapore has rendered for well over a century. Its role as the entrepot city of Southeast Asia, the marketplace of the region, will decrease in importance.

This is because Singapore is transforming itself into a new kind of city — a Global City. It is a new form of human organization and settlement that has, as the historian Arnold Toynbee says, no precedent in mankind's past history. People have become aware of this new type of city only very recently. They have found a name for this distinctive type of city. They call it Ecumenopolis — the world-embracing city.

It is this global character which distinguishes Ecumenopolis or the World City from the cities of the past. Earlier, cities were isolated centers of local civilizations and regional empires. They were, in comparison with global cities, somewhat parochial, with an extremely limited range of influence. They were capital cities of prestige, holy cities, city-states, or even capitals of convenience.

But the Global City, now in its infancy, is the child of modern technology. It is the city that electronic communications, supersonic planes, giant tankers and modern economic and industrial organization have made inevitable. Whether the Global City will be a happier place than the megalopolis out of whose crumbling ruins it is emerging will depend on how wisely and boldly we shape its direction and growth.

By and large, men have made a mess of their cities. They have yet to learn how to cope with cities. In the West and more so in Asia, most cities are unpleasant places to live in. Many of them are dirty, crime-ridden, anarchic and often violence prone. In many Western cities, the trend is for the well-to-do minority to flee to the outskirts of cities, while the rural poor swarm into the heart of the already congested cities.

One writer has described this process as the conversion of many a once-proud metropolis into a necropolis — a dumping ground for unwanted motor cars and unwanted human beings.

Whether cities are good or bad, the trend towards urbanization is irreversible. Individual cities may decay and eventually pass out of history. But since remote times, however much we may denounce them, the cities have been the creators and sustainers of civilization, culture, technology and wealth. The slogan about the countryside surrounding the cities is no more than the defiant cry of agrarian romantics as they watch the countryside being swallowed up relentlessly by the cities. This process has been accelerated cataclysmically in Asia since World War II.

Population in Asian cities has doubled and even tripled during the past decade. Nearly two-thirds of the world's increase in urban population during the past decade took place in the Third World. Nearly half the world's population today lives in cities. The coming decades will see the further urbanization of the world's population. For most of Asia, this uncontrolled growth of cities is posing serious social, economic and political problems.

But nothing short of a total collapse of world civilization can halt the takeover of the world by the cities.

Global Cities Interlinked

It is against this background that the Global City should be viewed. The Global Cities, unlike earlier cities, are linked intimately with one another. Because they are more alike, they reach out to one another through the tentacles of technology. Linked together, they form a chain of cities which today shape and direct, in varying degrees of importance, a worldwide system of economics. It is my contention that Singapore is becoming a component of that system — not a major component, but a growingly important one. It is in this sense that I have chosen to describe Singapore as a Global City.

That is why all the gloomy predictions about the future of an independent Singapore have been proved wrong. The pessimistic scenario was written on the assumption that an independent Singapore would be a self-contained city-state; that it would, at the most, be a regional city, and therefore its fate and fortunes would depend wholly on the economic climate in the region. The economic climate of the region is no doubt important to us and what happens in the region would have consequences for us economically, politically and militarily.

But we are more than a regional city. We draw sustenance not only from the region, but also from the international economic system to which as a Global City we belong and which will be the final arbiter of whether we prosper or decline.

If we view Singapore's future not as a regional city but as a Global City, then the smallness of Singapore, the absence of a hinterland or raw materials and a large domestic market are not fatal or insurmountable handicaps. It would explain why, since independence, we have been successful economically and, consequently, have ensured political and social stability.

Let me, as an example, deal with the question of hinterland. We have, it is true, no hinterland of our own. Were we a self-contained regional city and nothing more, we would today be in serious trouble.

But once you see Singapore as a Global City, the problem of hinterland becomes unimportant because for a Global City, the world is its hinterland. This is no hopeful theory. Our shipping statistics show clearly that the world is our hinterland. In 1959, some 9,500 ships brought 14 million tons of cargo to Singapore. Some ten years later, in 1970, the number of ships had doubled and the cargo trebled. The ships came from all parts of the world, carrying goods to and from all parts of the world.

Our port is not merely a regional port, but a global port. Our port makes the world its hinterland. We can get all the raw materials we lack cheaply and quickly because the sea remains the most economic way of transporting bulk cargo. You do not have to spend vast sums of money building roads and railroads to open up the sea. The sea is all highway. All you need is a ship to get to Singapore. The sea gives us ready access to other Global Cities.

Singapore is linked in other ways to other Global Cities. We are in constant and instantaneous contact, through cable and satellite communications, with some 140 countries.

We are also linked by air. Some 24 international airlines operate scheduled services to most parts of the world. In 1970, there were slightly over 17,000 landings at our airport — almost treble the number in 1960.

Some 521,000 visitors passed through Singapore, some for pleasure and others on business, in 1970.

We can best visualize the extent to which Singapore has become a Global City by tracing on a map the daily movements of aircraft and ships, the contacts made by telephone, cable, external trade and money transactions. Such a map would show how closely and increasingly we are being linked to other Global Cities. Each technological breakthrough in communications media annihilates distance and brings us closer to other Global Cities. We, like other Global Cities, are getting nearer. A Singaporean can get to Hong Kong quicker than he can to Kuala Lipis. His major trading partners are the other Global Cities rather than cities near home. We can, via the satellite, see and hear on our television events in London, Tokyo or Jakarta a split second after they happen.

Singapore's claim to being a Global City does not rest on its communications network alone.

We are also being connected to other Global Cities through the international financial network. We have become an important gold market center. The Asian dollar market has become an important aspect of our banking system. When the market was first established, most of its funds were reinvested in Euro dollars or US dollars in Europe and the United States. But now, a growing number of companies in Southeast Asia have taken to borrowing from the Asian dollar market. The funds which in 1970 stood at $1,200 million are now being increasingly used to finance business and projects in the region. The establishment in Singapore of a still growing number of foreign banks and merchant banks whose operations are worldwide is yet another indication of the fact that we are becoming a Global City.

The strongest evidence of Singapore's absorption into the emerging system of Global Cities is its link-up, more and more, with international and multinational corporations. We have been aware for a long time that consumption is no longer wholly a national matter. Economic nationalism has not prevented people from buying and consuming goods from all parts of the world.

But now, production itself is becoming an international operation. The conventional idea that goods move internationally but that factors of production do not, is being eroded by new realities. Internationalization of production through the worldwide expansion of international and multinational corporations is moving forward at an amazing speed. As far back as 1968, it was noted that the growth rate of internationalized production exceeded the growth rate of the vast majority of nations and far exceeded the growth rate of their exports. In the same year, the total output of all foreign affiliates of American corporations was four times the total American exports for that year. Foreign production of US firms has been growing twice as fast as the domestic economy.

In fact, the American international and multinational corporations abroad have been described as the third largest economy in the world after the United States and the Soviet Union.

Internationalized production is only in its infancy. At the moment, the Americans are in the vanguard of this movement, though in certain sectors of internationalized production the Europeans are equally prominent. But whatever the final shape of internationalized production, it will be the major channel of international trade, commerce and production in the decades ahead.

By linking up with international and multinational corporations, Singapore not only becomes a component of world economy, but is offered a shortcut to catch up or at least keep pace with the most advanced industrial and technological societies. By plugging-in in this way, we can achieve in 20 to 30 years what otherwise would have taken us a century or more to achieve.

This is because the international and multinational corporations introduce us to high technology, complex managerial and marketing skills, in addition to bringing in investments. They start complex industries for which we have neither the capital resources nor the expertise to initiate ourselves. Whether the host countries can absorb and utilize the opportunities offered will depend on whether the people concerned respond rationally or irrationally to these mammoth and occasionally unfeeling institutions.

There are admittedly grave political and economic dangers implicit in the entry of powerful foreign concerns into weak and underdeveloped countries. I believe that many of the men who control these big concerns from remote Global Cities are not idealists. They may not even understand that the institutions they have created may be powerful instruments for shaping the world economy or vastly shrunken world demands.

But Singapore must be prepared to run these risks simply because the alternative to not moving into the global economic system is, for small Singapore, certain ruin. We can, if we have the will and the intelligence, create the necessary antibodies within our social system to give us immunity against the many dangers that close association with giant foreign corporations could pose.

But they also provide, as I said, shortcuts to enable us to catch up with the advanced societies. It will ensure that when the 21st century dawns, those Singaporeans living then would be men of the 21st century — this means well over half the Singaporeans now living.

As a matter of fact, we are already plugged into the 21st century through these foreign corporations. In manufacturing, which is the leading growth sector of our economy, the more substantial investments have come from international and multinational corporations. Most of the $1,700 million now invested in industries have come from international firms. Their presence will partly explain how Singapore has been able to expand industrially despite its small domestic market. The reason is that these international and multinational concerns simultaneously bring with them not only industries, but also established markets. For these firms, the world is their hinterland; the world is their market and through them we are automatically linked to the global hinterland and world markets that would, on our own, have not been available to us.

I hope I have elucidated somewhat the mystery of why an independent Singapore, far from collapsing as many expected, continues to make progress. The gist of this possibly lengthy discourse is that an independent Singapore survives and will survive because it has established a relationship of interdependence in the rapidly expanding global economic system. Singapore's economic future will, as the years go by, become more and more rooted in this global system. It will grow and prosper with it.

In this address, I have dealt largely with the economic aspects of Singapore as a Global City. But the political, social and cultural implications of being a Global City are no less important. I have not dealt with them simply because my talk would have been five times as long. The political, social and cultural problems, I believe, would be far more difficult to tackle. These may be the Achilles' heel of the emerging Global Cities.

Laying the economic infrastructure of a Global City may turn out to be the easiest of the many tasks involved in creating such a city. But the political, social and cultural adjustments such a city would require to enable men to live happy and useful lives in them may demand a measure of courage, imagination and intelligence which may or may not be beyond the capacity of its citizens.

For those people who cannot develop the necessary capacities, the Global City may turn out to be another monster — another necropolis.

So it is up to us to equip our people intellectually and spiritually to make the Global City into the Heavenly City that prophets and seers have dreamt about since time immemorial.

Talk by Mr S. Dhanabalan, Minister for Foreign Affairs, at the NUS Forum at Lecture Theatre No. 11, Singapore, November 27, 1981

To understand the precepts and purposes of Singapore's foreign policy, it will be necessary for me to go back a little into history, if only to show the nature and realities of international politics and the impact they have had on the environment in which Singapore exists.

The fundamental precepts of our foreign policy are clear:

— We will be friends with all who wish to be friends with us;
— We will trade with any state for mutual benefit, regardless of ideology or system of government;
— We will remain non-aligned with regard to the rivalries of great-power blocs;
— We will cooperate closely with ASEAN members to achieve regional cohesion, stability and progress.

These precepts, formulated in the initial years of our independence, have guided us safely so far. There are no reasons to abandon them. But as we face new realities, we have to modify, change emphasis and adapt these precepts.

New Realities

More than 30 years ago, as that dust settled on the debris of the Second World War, it was evident that a fundamental re-structuring of global power had occurred. Europe lay prostrate after the strain of overthrowing Hitler. The USSR, though victorious with the help of the allies, had suffered severe damage and, though in the Red Army it still possessed an awesome instrument, its reach was limited to cannon range. China was seized by the throes of a civil war; a great power only by courtesy. It was plain that the US had emerged politically, economically and militarily superior to all its rivals. This would remain so for many years.

We describe the international system of the 1950s and the early 1960s as "Bipolar", but it was a bipolarity in which the US was clearly dominant. It was indeed, the very magnitude of its dominance that enabled the US to conceive of, and then to sustain, an ambitious global policy of "containment" of militant Communist powers.

The growing American involvement in Southeast Asia was one facet of its global policy of "containment" of Communism. After the outbreak of the Korean War, the US came to perceive the stabilization of Southeast Asia and, in particular, the preservation of the integrity of South Vietnam, as an essential component of this policy.

Throughout the 1950s and the early 1960s, the Southeast Asian regional balance of power thus mirrored America's global dominance. As the European colonial powers receded and gradually gave effect to their policy of withdrawal from Southeast Asia, the US presence swelled to fill the void. By the time Singapore gained independence in 1965, America was the single most important element of the regional power structure. Britain, while still a significant power in the region, only played a subsidiary and supportive role.

In Indochina, the Soviet Union, China and the US were engaged in a struggle that was, as yet, clearly unequal. The Soviet Union, lacking the ability to project its power, was not seen as a clear threat and was only beginning to be considered in the calculations of regional states. China was a source of concern only because of its commitment to export revolution and because of its support for the insurgencies in the non-Communist states of the region. We in Singapore, like the others in the region, were certainly aware of the ominous rumblings to our North, but there was no pressing fear of imminent danger.

By the beginning of the 1970s, it was clear that the international system was changing yet again, and by the end of the decade an unmistakably new structure was emerging. American power waned while Soviet power waxed; China began to emerge from the self-imposed isolation of the Cultural Revolution; British withdrawal East of Suez was an accomplished fact; West Europe and Japan acquired new status as global economic powers; *detente* began to be seriously thought of, though by the end of the decade it appeared to have slipped into a coma; Sino-Soviet conflict took on new and more threatening dimensions; the US withdrew from Indochina; North Vietnam invaded and annexed South Vietnam and fulfilled its 30-year dream of reunification; Sino-American relations were normalized and Sino-Vietnamese relations soured; Vietnam launched into hegemonistic adventures in Laos and Cambodia.

These events, and others, are more than a series of discrete occurences. In their totality, they have changed the structure of the international system.

There will never again be a situation in Southeast Asia or any other region where the US will be the only power of significance. The Soviet Union will not disappear nor can the growth of China's influence be prevented. Our region has become a tripolar region, with a galaxy of regional powers associated with one or the other big powers. It is in this context that Singapore's foreign policy or diplomacy will have to be conducted.

This tripolar structure, and the consequent modification of the rules-of-the-game, was the primary new reality that our foreign policy had to grapple with. With these changes, Singapore has had to devise qualitatively new approaches in the conduct of diplomacy while, at the same time, preserving the fundamental precepts of our foreign policy.

New Challenges

How has this structural change been manifested in our region in recent times? What are the new rules-of-the-game?

In Southeast Asia, the particular challenge engendered by the new structure of power has been the arrival of the Soviet Union as a power in the region through a united Communist Vietnam. As long as the US was the predominant power in the region, the non-Communist Southeast Asian states were insulated from the instabilities of Indochina. US military forces in Thailand and South Vietnam served as a buffer against the threat of externally assisted Communist "People's War" spreading to other parts of Southeast Asia. This enabled us and others in the region to pursue our separate paths of political and economic development without undue disruption from the storms raging to the north. Moreover, with the US underwriting the sovereignty of South Vietnam against a Communist takeover by armed invasion, the non-Communist states of the region were able to avoid having to come to terms with any threats arising from a powerful and united Communist Vietnam — a Vietnam committed to support the overthrow of established governments through violent revolution.

With the removal of the American buffer, this comfortable state of affairs evaporated. We and our ASEAN partners began the process of developing some kind of *modus vivendi* with an ideologically hostile neighbour whose military strength far outweighed our combined strength. We faced distressing questions about the nature and limits of Hanoi's ambitions and the possible effect of their success on the threat posed by communist insurgencies in the ASEAN states.

ASEAN's initial response to the fall of South Vietnam was a cautious one. Attempts were made to establish some form of *detente* with Hanoi. The ASEAN Foreign Ministers Conferences held in Kuala Lumpur in May 1975 symbolized this attempt. ASEAN expressed its "readiness to enter into friendly and harmonious relationships with each nation in Indochina" and a "willingness to cooperate with these countries in the common task of national development". This offer was initially greeted with a vehement rebuff. However, by the end of 1976, we began to meet with some measure of success, interspersed with differenced arising from Vietnam's call for genuine independence of the countries of non-Communist Southeast Asia. By the end of 1978, with the Vietnamese Prime Minister, Mr Pham Van Dong's fairly amicable tour of ASEAN capitals, we thought a new phase of co-existence with the prospects of cooperation and amity had arrived.

The Vietnamese invasion of Cambodia swept away the beginning of this precarious *detente* and brought forth new concerns. The invasion was clearly in contravention of assurances that we had received from the Vietnamese Prime Minister only a few months previously. Further, it sought to establish a new principle in international relations, i.e., that a country had the right to intervene militarily and overthrow the established government of a neighbouring country just because it did not approve of that government's conduct in its own country. But more ominous was the role that the Soviet Union played in this event. Having acquired the ability to project its power into Southeast Asia, the Soviet Union demonstrated that it was willing to underwrite Vietnamese aggression against neighbouring states. As Vietnamese tanks rolled into Phnom Penh, Chinese troops also poured across the Sino-Vietnamese border. We thus witnessed, at first hand, the alarming consequences of the new elements in the regional structure of power and how each was prepared to use its power to promote its interest. The Southeast Asian balance of power seemed to be spinning out of control.

New Rules-of-the-Game

To have acquiesced would have been to court disaster, for to allow aggression to go unchecked or unprotested is only to invite further aggression. But how were we to respond?

During the earlier period of American presence in Southeast Asia, our foreign policy had been essentially passive. Under the then prevailing conditions, a passive foreign policy was the most prudent one. It was unnecessary for us to actively seek a high profile and unwise to draw unnecessary attention by seeking to play a role which we could not have successfully sustained.

Under the new rules-of-the-game, this was no longer a viable option. In a situation where the predominance of a single great power was replaced by the contention of several great powers in a fluid, shifting balance of power, a quiescent foreign policy was a standing invitation to disaster. To crouch still in the hope of remaining unnoticed, and thus unthreatened, was only to risk being trampled upon. Nor could we find security by seeking the protection of one or the other of the big powers. No power, big or small, can be a reliable steward of any interest but its own.

When the gods of international polities contend, they help only those who help themselves. History is littered with the rubble of states who have lacked the will to take their fate into their own hands.

New Directions

Accordingly, we embarked on a new and more activist course. On the Cambodian question, we sought to achieve our fundamental aims not simply by acquiescing in, and reacting to, events, but by attempting to shape events to our purposes. Our new course encompasses:

—Working with any state, irrespective of ideology, whose interests at any time coincide with Singapore's interests;

—Rallying international support for Singapore's causes;

—Rallying support for the worthy causes of other nations which have supported Singapore and whose causes are not harmful to Singapore's interests.

We have not embarked on this course alone, but with the other ASEAN states. It is hardly necessary for me to stress the fact that co-operation with our ASEAN partners on issues of mutual concern lies at the very centre of Singapore's foreign policy.

ASEAN's Achievement

In ASEAN, working with Thailand, Malaysia, Indonesia and the Philippines, we have forged an instrument of increasing international repute; we are recognised as a cohesive entity by all the major powers of the world — even the Soviet Union for example pays us the left-handed compliment of labelling us a "bloc" which it does its best to divide. We are consulted on issues affecting Southeast Asia and play an effective role in international forums.

ASEAN has succeeded in modifying established patterns of conflict and cooperation in Southeast Asia. The potentially most divisive disputes of the 1960s — Indonesia's "confrontation" of Malaysia, the Philippines claim to Sabah, the Thai-Malaysian and Indonesian-Philippines border disputes and the separation of Malaysia and Singapore — have all either became irrelevant or been muted considerably. Today, the ASEAN region is peaceful and unified. By contrast, the storms of war rage unabated in Communist Indochina, fallen under Vietnamese hegemony.

Criticisms

There are, of course, those who are critical of Singapore's ASEAN-orientated foreign policy and the more active role that we have adopted.

There are these who think that ASEAN makes too much of Cambodia; that the focus of our activities should be directed more on economic cooperation.

There are those who argue that ASEAN's unity is artificial; that we have emphasised areas of agreement but concealed existing differences.

And there are those who feel that, for a small country, Singapore had been too vocal; that we have taken public stands on issues that are of no direct concern to us and which we are powerless to influence or alter.

Let me take these points of view in turn.

It must be admitted, for example, that it would be preferable for ASEAN to focus its energies on economic cooperation rather than the Cambodian conflict. But it is entirely naive to believe that economic cooperation would have much chance of success in a situation of political instability. To have accepted Vietnam's occupation of Cambodia would have been to invite further aggressive probes.

On the second criticism, it must be clear that at any time, given limited resources, every state must choose between several possibilities of action, all worthy of equal attention. Foreign policy must therefore set priorities, and in ASEAN the priority is to nurture unity of perception and common interests.

The international system comprises sovereign states, each admitting to no authority except its own. International relations therefore resembles a Hobbesian state of nature, where each is pitted against all. In such a potentially anarchical situation, order is the prime value. In international politics, as in national politics, order is prior to justice, to morality, to economic prosperity, to any other value that you can think of simply because, in the absence of order, no other value can be realised. In the absence of order, the life of states would be as in the life of men in the state of nature — "Nasty, Brutish and Short".

International relations is thus a constant struggle to establish at least a modicum of order under conditions that are always threatening to lapse into anarchy. Any existing area of order, or cooperation, cannot therefore, be taken for granted but needs constant nurture. It is thus astounding that Singapore and other ASEAN states are criticised for emphasising their common interests rather than their areas of disagreement. Such critics betray such a startling ignorance of the nature of international political processes that one can only conclude that they are prompted by malice.

It is no secret that the five ASEAN states differ in their histories, their cultures, their economic systems, ethnic make-up and political institutions. But ASEAN's achievement is that these differences have been contained within the framework of the organization and that, as a result, the five states have been able to collaborate despite their disagreements. Sovereign states collaborate only when they perceive a mutual interest in collaboration. ASEAN has maintained its unity and progressed precisely because we have agreed not to emphasize our differences at the expense of our mutual interests. Open recriminations, and the inevitable inflammation of public opinion, would only divert attention from areas of agreed and existing cooperation.

To be sure, de-emphasising differences and disagreements does not solve them. We hope that, given time and as habits of cooperation become more deeply ingrained, our differences will be absorbed by an ever-expanding area of cooperation and mutual interest. But it is highly irresponsible to suggest that we should jeopardise our real achievements by airing our problems for the entertainment of journalists and political observers who will not bear any responsibility if ASEAN should fail.

The third criticism is, however, more substantial. It poses valid questions: what interests can a small state have in distant events? What influence can a small state have on international politics?

Power and Interdependence

If these questions had been posed in any other century, the answer to both could only have been "none". Traditional international politics consisted purely of a military-strategic game in which the only significant players were the great powers. Poor communication regionalized international politics; except for a handful of states whose interests and influence spanned oceans and continents, most states paid attention only to their immediate surroundings. Scant attention was paid to small states. But, as we come to the closing decades of the 20th century, it is clear that the answer would have to take cognizance of a series of complex developments in the international system and that a new type of international politics has emerged: The Politics of Interdependence.

In our time, a host of developments — the revolution in global communications, advances in weapons systems, new types of transport networks, the increase in the volume of international political and economic transactions, the explosion in the number of new states (most of which are small), the expansion of the subjects in the international agenda to include a wide range of economic issues as well as military-strategic questions, the growth of a global culture of modernity — these are but some of the more significant trends that have occurred. They have created, for the first time in history, a truly global international system; an interdependent international system; a world, not of isolated and autarkic regions, but of inter-locking parts where events anywhere have implications for events everywhere.

In such an interdependent world, technology has diminished the political significance of geographic distance. I have already described how the structure of the Southeast Asian regional balance of power has changed in response to changes in the international system. We cannot afford to ignore any event, however distant, that has the potential of affecting the power position or the relationships of the great powers.

This interdependence is often discussed. What is less commonly considered is the effect of this new type of international system on traditional notions of state power.

Traditional international politics was highly hierarchic, primarily because state power was measured by the size of armies and the level of their organization. Military power was important because firstly, military-strategic issues dominated the traditional international agenda; secondly, inter-state relations were most typically bilateral — a situation in which military power can most easily be brought to bear — and thirdly, there were few, if any, international constraints on the use of force.

Under conditions of interdependence, the importance of these conditions has become blurred. The result has been to complicate the hierarchic structure of international politics. There are new multiple hierarchies, with power varying according to the kind of issue at stake, and not being transferable from one issue-area to another. Thus, for example, the US has found it impossible to use its military strength to force the OPEC countries to lower their oil prices.

Another area of significant change is the growth in the number of international organisations and the great increase in the number of states. Today, an ever increasing number of international issues are being discussed and negotiated, not bilaterally, but multilaterally in the context of various international organisations. In part, this development has come about because, in an interdependent world where anything may affect everything, it makes little sense to discuss bilaterally issues that will affect all. The influence of international organisations is partly the result of the proliferation of new states, most of whom are small and weak, demanding a voice in world affairs. In international organisations, what counts is not size but votes. To be sure, the power of international organisations is limited, but the sheer number of new states ensures that no power, however great, can ignore them. International organisations thus do enjoy a degree of influence.

Finally, today, constraints on the use of force in international politics has increased. Not only does the jealousy of the great powers check each ability to use force against the friends or potential friends of the other, but the existence of accepted legal prohibitions against the use of force in the UN Charter and elsewhere ensures that, if states will not renounce force as an instrument of policy, they can only resort to force with a bad conscience. They have to seek to justify its use or represent it in terms which they believe will be acceptable to the uninitiated and the disinterested. For instance, the Soviets claim that they are only extending "friendly assistance" to Afghanistan or Vietnam's position is that it is an invited guest in Cambodia. The need to justify is itself one kind of constraint.

These developments have complicated traditional notions of state power. Military forces and size are still important, but they are no longer the only important criteria. I have dwelt at some length on these developments because they form the reasoning behind our new foreign policy orientation. It is important for us not only to know what we need to do in the field of international relations, but why we have to do it and how we go about doing it. I believe that Singapore, despite its small size, can influence international developments by:

— Narrowing our attention to specific issues which directly affect our security;
— Keeping abreast of developments and securing and using information on the issue in question;
— Carefully selecting the time, place and forum in which we want to make our case on the issue.

None of these are traditional power resources, but using these means, Singapore and our partners in ASEAN have been able to acquire a degree of international influence that bears no relation to our size. Let me illustrate this by references to the most pressing issue on our agenda, the crisis in Cambodia.

Firstly, choosing the forum. Had we chosen to deal with Cambodia as an issue involving ASEAN and Vietnam alone, we would have missed the international implications of the problem arising from the involvement of powers outside the region. We would have had no opportunity to mobilise political and diplomatic opinion to counter Vietnam's military superiority. Our choice would have been either to accept Vietnamese *fait accompli* or a bilateral confrontation in which ASEAN could only come out second-best.

Instead we chose to take the issue to the UN. Firstly, because of the international character of the problem and, secondly, to mobilise as large a group of supporters as could be marshalled to put political pressure on Vietnam, her patron and her allies. In the UN we capitalised on ASEAN's international stature and the willingness of other states to listen to our point of view. In the UN we were spared the stark choice of acquiescence or confrontation and were instead able to force the Vietnamese to choose between withdrawal or international political isolation and deprivation of international aid. The overwhelming support that ASEAN obtained in the UN has stiffened the resolve of friendly developed countries to step up political and economic pressure on Vietnam, thus making Vietnam pay a telling price.

I stressed the need for information. Knowledge is power because without the guidance of knowledge, action is ineffective. In an inter-dependent world, the sheer volume of communication flows means that no state can muster all information on every issue.

States are forced to rely on each other for information on particular issues.

Our UN strategy was successful because we were able to secure and use information effectively. By carefully monitoring developments in Cambodia, ASEAN was able to put forth information about develop-ments in that country and their implications for states unfamiliar with the details of the issue. By our use of the information on the issue we were able to persuade others to understand the ramifications of the Cambodian question for them and see the justification to support our position. Here again we were invaluably aided by the international repute that ASEAN has acquired. For most states, we are a more cred-ible source of information on the issue than Vietnam or its allies.

Finally, the ability to pay attention to particular issues is also a power resource. In an inter-dependent world, the sheer range and number of issues that demand the attention of states is overwhelming. The greater its power and the wider its interests are spread, the more difficult it will be for a state to pay adequate attention to every issue that is brought to its notice. Thus, with respect to issues on the periphery of their vision, states tend to take their one from those to whom these issues are cen-tral. In this respect, small states who are able to devote their full atten-tion to a narrow range of issues can be quite influential on particular subjects.

Because Cambodia is so important to ASEAN, we devoted most of our energies to it and, by doing so, were able to lead other states in our direction.

ASEAN's strategy on the Cambodian issue illustrates the political processes of global interdependence and the ability of small states to muster influence in the new international politics. By those means we have succeeded in keeping the issue alive, preventing Vietnam from claiming a *fait accompli*; we have isolated Vietnam politically and eco-nomically; we have convened an international conference on Cambodia and used the conference to elaborate the principles and mechanisms of a future political settlement to the Cambodian crisis; and we have done this in the face of pressure from great powers opposed to our course. To some, this may not seem very much, but it is perhaps more than what the small powers would have dared to dream of achieving in the past.

Yet, even as I enumerate our successes and extol the international politics of interdependence, I would be shirking my responsibility if I did not also recognise the limits to our possibilities of influence. The new international politics has not displaced traditional international politics but only complicated it. The fact remains that military strength is still important and we would be unrealistic if we did not acknowledge this fact. In international affairs, others who are opposed to you will always judge your diplomacy by the underpinning of your defence capability. Likewise, defence can only be sustained in an inter-dependent world by the quality and strength of your foreign policy or diplomacy.

But realism in international politics consists not only of acknowl-edging limits but also of recognising opportunities. Between what presently exists and what we must ultimately accept lies a margin of possibilities. It is within this margin that we operate. It is within this margin that we must seek out those opportunities that will assure our future.

The conduct of foreign policy is like navigating a ship through dan-gerous waters. Our fundamental aim is, and will remain, to avoid ship-wreck. But, as we proceed in the 1980s, changes in the structure and processes of international politics have given us the opportunity, as well as made it necessary, to steer a more positive course. We cannot be solely at the mercy of the tides and the winds. History will not forgive us if we do so.

Speech by Tommy Koh at the School of Foreign Service, Georgetown University, USA, November 18, 1987

Can Any Country Afford a Moral Foreign Policy?

This is the text of a speech given by Tommy Koh at Georgetown University on November 18, 1987 on being presented with the 1987 Jit Trainor Award for Distinction in the Conduct of Diplomacy.

Source: Koh, Tommy T.B., *The Quest for World Order: Perspectives of a Pragmatic Idealist*, Amitav Acharya, ed., Singapore, Times Academic Press for Institute of Policy Studies, 1998.

Let me begin with a caveat and a confession. The caveat is that the views I am about to express are my own and do not necessarily reflect those of my government. The confession is that although I have spent more than 16 years in the foreign service of my country, I regard myself as an amateur in diplomacy. My formal education was in law, a fact which some adherents of the Realist school of foreign policy would regard as a disqualification rather than a qualification. I did not have the benefit of having attended a school of foreign service, such as this, or of having studied political science or international relations. I did not work my way up the ladder of my country's foreign service. Instead, I was helicoptered to the top of the ladder at a comparatively young age. I have been learning on the job. What follows is an account of a personal odyssey; the reflections of an untutored practitioner of the craft of diplomacy and an attempt to develop a framework encompassing the role of power and force, of morality and law, of conflict and negotiation in the conduct of foreign policy.

> *It is necessary ... to be a great pretender and dissembler ... he who seeks to deceive will always find someone who will allow himself to be deceived.* (Machiavelli)

I arrived at the United Nations in New York in August 1968. A few days after my arrival, Soviet and other Warsaw Pact forces invaded Czechoslovakia and put an end to Alexander Dubcek's reform movement. On the instructions of his government, the head of the Czechoslovak delegation requested an urgent meeting of the UN Security Council and demanded the immediate withdrawal of the invading forces. During the meetings of the Security Council, the Soviet Ambassador first denied that his country had invaded Czechoslovakia. I was astonished both by his ability to tell a pack of lies with apparent sincerity and by the stupidity of his action. No one in the UN was taken in by his deceit. In December 1978, Vietnam invaded Cambodia. At first, the Vietnamese Ambassador also sought to deny that his country had invaded Cambodia. In December 1979, the Soviet Union invaded Afghanistan. Initially, the Soviet Ambassador attempted to deny the invasion. The propensity by governments and their diplomatic agents to lie is not confined to the communist countries. In my 13 years at the UN, I was appalled by the duplicitous conduct of colleagues from all parts of the world. Is it any wonder that jokesters like to say that diplomats are individuals who are sent abroad to lie for their country?

Machiavelli, in his classic work, *The Prince*, said that "he who seeks to deceive will always find someone who will allow himself to be deceived."[1] In my experience, Machiavelli's assertion is untrue. No one at the UN was deceived by the lies of my errant colleagues. In the contemporary world of instantaneous communication, of an alert and probing world press, of satellite monitoring, it is futile to lie. The truth will prevail over falsehood. Apart from a few gullible people

---

[1] Nicolo Machiavelli, *The Prince*, Everyman's Library, Ernst Page, ed., New York, E.P. Dutton & Co., 1952, p. 143.

and those who wear ideological blinkers, most people are not easily deceived.

Machiavelli also advised the prince that "It is necessary to be a great pretender and dissembler".[2] In my experience, this is bad advice. In the community of nations, some governments and diplomats acquire a reputation for duplicity and dishonesty. Is a government or a diplomat with a reputation for veracity and integrity more likely to succeed in promoting the country's interests than one with a reputation for duplicity? I think the answer is yes. I have witnessed at the UN that governments and diplomats with a reputation for veracity and integrity tend to enjoy more influence and stature and are more likely to be entrusted with leadership positions than governments and diplomats with dubious reputations. Sissela Bok was right to have pointed out in her book, *Lying: Moral Choice in Public and Private Life*, that "Trust and integrity are precious resources."[3]

> *Whether, to consummate their enterprise, have they to use prayers or can they use force? In the first instance they always succeed badly, and never compass anything; but when they can rely on themselves and use force, then they are rarely endangered.*[4] (Machiavelli)

The Nuremburg Trials have made the waging of wars of aggression a crime against humanity. The Charter of the United Nations has prohibited the use of force except in self-defence. Notwithstanding these achievements in international law and in the evolving international consensus on the norms applicable to relations between states, violence and conflict are the ugly realities of our contemporary world. In view of this, it could be asked whether Machiavelli's advice to the prince to use force to consummate his enterprise is as valid today as it was 500 years ago?

Are there any limits to the efficiency of the use of force in the modern world? Let us examine this question in respect of the relations

---

[2] *Ibid.*, p. 142.

[3] Sissela Bok, *Lying: Moral Choice in Public and Private Life*, New York, Pantheon Books, 1978, p. 249.

[4] Machiavelli, *op. cit.*, p. 48.

between the two superpowers, between a nuclear power and a non-nuclear power and between two non-nuclear powers. In the relations between the two superpowers, the doctrine of mutual assured destruction has practically precluded either power from resorting to force in settling disputes with the other. Both President Reagan and General Secretary Gorbachev agree that nuclear wars cannot be won and must never be fought. It is unlikely for either power to start a conventional war against the other because such a war is likely to escalate into a nuclear war.

Let us turn to look at the conflict in Afghanistan as an example of a nuclear power using force to subjugate a non-nuclear power. In spite of the Soviet Union's preponderance in firepower, it has been unable to subjugate the guerrilla forces of the Mujahideen. What lessons can one learn from Afghanistan regarding the efficacy of the use of force? First, that a tenacious guerrilla army can neutralize, to some extent, the difference in the firepower of the armies of a nuclear power and a non-nuclear power. Second, that although the international system is too weak to prevent aggression, it is capable of inflicting political and economic costs on the aggressor. The invasion of Afghanistan has diminished the influence of the Soviet Union with the members of the Non-Aligned Movement and the Organization of Islamic Conference (OIC). At the current session of the UN General Assembly, 123 states voted against the Soviet Union on Afghanistan. Third, that even a totalitarian state which professes to be unaffected by the opinion of mankind must be concerned by its standing in the eyes of the other states in the international community. General Secretary Gorbachev is reported to be anxious to find a diplomatic formula which would enable him to pull Soviet troops out of Afghanistan.

The same lessons are applicable to the case of Vietnam's invasion of Cambodia, an example of a non-nuclear power resorting to force to subjugate another non-nuclear power. The tenacity of the resistance plus the political and economic isolation of Vietnam are beginning to have an impact on the policy-makers in Hanoi. Between 1975 and 1978, Vietnam was treated like a heroic nation, especially by the non-aligned countries. Today, Vietnam is an isolated nation. I do not believe that this dramatic change in the standing of Vietnam in the world community has had no effect on the leaders of the politburo in Hanoi. Indeed, there are signs to suggest that Vietnam's leaders may soon be ready to consider non-military options to end the conflict in Cambodia.

The purpose of this excursus is not to assert the proposition that in the modern world states can never succeed in using force to achieve their ends. The Soviet Union has, for example, succeeded in subjugating Hungary and Czechoslovakia. Other states have also succeeded in using force to occupy parts of their neighbours' territories and in incorporating foreign territories and peoples within their boundaries. The purpose of this excursus is to question the Machiavellian thesis that a state can always rely upon its superior force to consummate its enterprise. There are clearly limits to the efficacy of the use of force in the contemporary world, limits imposed by the nature of nuclear war, by the character of guerrilla war, by the political and economic costs which the international system, weak as it is, is capable of inflicting on the aggressor and, in the case of democratic societies, by domestic public opinion.

Saints can be pure, but statesmen must be responsible. As trustees for others, they must defend interests and compromise principles.[5] (Arthur Schlesinger)

In his celebrated book, *Moral Man and Immoral Society*, the Christian theologian, Reinhold Niebuhr, wrote that "Perhaps the most significant moral characteristic of a nation is its hypocrisy."[6] In *The Cycles of American History*, Arthur Schlesinger said that "Saints can be pure, but statesmen must be responsible. As trustees for others, they must defend interests and compromise principles".[7] Both Niebuhr and Schlesinger belong to the Realist school of foreign policy. They believe that the lodestar which guides a state in the conduct of its foreign policy is its national interest. But, does it follow that in pursuing its

---

[5] Arthur M. Schlesinger, *The Cycles of American History*, Boston, Houghton Mifflin, 1986, p. 72.

[6] Reinhold Niebuhr, *Moral Man and Immoral Society*, New York, Charles Scribner & Sons, 1932, p. 95.

[7] Schlesinger, *op. cit.*

national interest, a state must be hypocritical, that it must compromise its principles? Let me explore these questions by reference to the following examples.

The first example revolves around the principle of self-determination. Spanish Sahara was a Spanish colony in North-West Africa, situated between Morocco and Mauritania. In order to pressurize Spain into decolonizing the territory, the African group at the UN asked the International Court of Justice for an advisory opinion on the right of the people of Spanish Sahara to self-determination. The court upheld the right of the people of the Spanish colony to freedom and independence. Acting contrary to the opinion of the court, Morocco and Mauritania occupied the colony and divided it between them. (Mauritania later gave up its share of the territory.) When the question came before the UN General Assembly, the then US Ambassador to the UN lobbied me to support Morocco, arguing that Morocco had always supported Singapore's and ASEAN's interests whereas Algeria (which supported the pro-independence movement in Spanish Sahara — Polisario) had not always done so. The argument was factually correct. I pointed out, however, that what was at issue was not whether Algeria or Morocco was a better friend of Singapore, but the principle of self-determination which was important to small countries such as Singapore. I explained that it was contrary to Singapore's national interest to undermine that principle. I argued that Singapore's credibility would be eroded if it failed to stand up for the principle against all violations. Therefore, I concluded that Singapore's long-term national interest was better served by supporting the principle of self-determination than by supporting a friend. I appreciate that the yardstick of national interest is imprecise and reasonable. People can disagree as to what course of action is most consonant with a country's interest.

My next example concerns the US intervention in Grenada. For small countries such as Singapore, one of the most precise principles of international law and international relations is the principle of non-interference in the internal affairs of other states. The intervention by the United States, Barbados, Jamaica and the members of the Organization of Eastern Caribbean States (OECS) in Grenada posed a dilemma for me. On the one hand, I appreciated that the motive which led those states to intervene was a benign one, i.e., to rescue the people of Grenada from an oppressive communist regime and to return the country to democracy. On the other hand, the intervention was contrary to the Charter of the United Nations and to international law. I also realized that if I had not protested against the intervention in Grenada, it would have undermined my moral credibility in leading the opposition to the Soviet intervention in Afghanistan and the Vietnamese intervention in Cambodia. After wrestling with the dilemma, I came to the conclusion that the national interest of Singapore required that I put principle ahead of friendship. This is what I said to the Security Council:

> *Mr President, it is easy enough for us to demonstrate our adherence to principle when to do so is convenient and advantageous and costs us nothing. The test of a country's adherence to principle is when it is inconvenient to do so. I find myself in such a situation today. Barbados, Jamaica, the United States and the member states of the OECS are friends of my country. It is extremely convenient for me to acquiesce in what they have done or to remain silent. To do so, however, will, in the long run, undermine the moral and legal significance of the principles which my country regards as a shield. This is why we must put our adherence to principle above friendship. This is why we cannot condone the action of our friends in Grenada. The stand which my country has taken in this case is consistent with the stand which we have taken in other cases where the principle of non-interference in the international affairs of states was also violated.*

Let me bring this discussion to a close. What is my lodestar? Do I subscribe to the Realist or the Moralist school of foreign policy? I reject the Realist school not because of its moral cynicism but because it does not reflect the world in which we live. The Realists believe that the only standard by which a state should conduct its foreign policy is its national interest. They believe that in pursuit of its national interest, it is necessary for a state to be hypocritical and to compromise its principles. They reject any consideration of ethics or morality in the conduct of foreign policy as being irrelevant. Although they do not say so expressly, the logical implication of the Realist stand is that we live in a world of anomie, that is to say, in a condition of lawlessness, in the absence of any governing structure, in a situation in which there are no laws, principles, rules to govern the conduct between nations. Is this an accurate description of the world in which we live?

In my view it is not. We live in an imperfect world. It is not, however, a lawless world. The world community has evolved by custom, and adopted by treaty, a very considerable body of laws, principles and rules to govern the conduct between states as well as between states and their citizens. This body of international law deals with almost every area of international relations, including the recognition of states and their admission to international organizations; trade and foreign investment; diplomatic protection of nationals; nationality; war; human rights; boundaries; territorial acquisition; the law of the oceans. There are therefore universally accepted criteria by which the conduct of a state may be judged to be lawful or unlawful, right or wrong. The Realists will say, at this point, that there is a big difference between international law and domestic law. Domestic law works because it is a command backed up by force. There is no force behind the decisions of the International Court of Justice or the UN Security Council. In his book, *International Conflict for Beginners*, Roger Fisher answered the argument in the following way:

> *The [US] Supreme Court had no regiments at its command. It had no greater force vis-à-vis the government than does the International Court of Justice sitting at the Hague.*[8]

> *Law enforcement against a government involves not a command backed up by force. Rather it involves so changing the choice with which the government is confronted that their long-range interest in orderly settlement of disputes outweighs their short-run interest in winning this particular dispute.*[9]

I agree with Roger Fisher that the Realist tends to exaggerate the difference between domestic law and international law. However, I concede that international law does not have the same efficacy as domestic law in a well-ordered society. Although the international legal system is weak, it is not totally ineffective. I also feel that the

---

[8] Roger Fisher, *International Conflict for Beginners*, London, Allen Lane, 1971, p. 155.
[9] *Ibid.*, p. 156.

Realist view that in the conduct of its foreign policy, a state should act exclusively on the basis of its national interest is flawed because, in reality, no state, no matter how powerful, can entirely ignore the interests of other states, the rules of international law and international relations, the decisions and recommendations of international, regional and binational institutions and the opinion of mankind.

However, my rejection of the Realist school does not lead me to embrace the Moralist school. What is the Moralist view of foreign policy? The Moralist believes that moral values should control foreign policy. He believes that no matter how noble and virtuous the end, it never justifies the use of means that violate moral or ethical standards. Some moralists have argued that states should behave in accordance with the same high standards of morality that apply to individuals in a good society.

I have a major problem with the Moralist school. The Moralist fails to appreciate that the primary purpose of a government is to protect the independence, sovereignty and territorial integrity of the state and to promote the welfare of its people. In pursuing these objectives, a government ought to employ means which are lawful and moral. However, there will be situations, hopefully rare, when a government will be confronted by conflicts between its national interest and its fidelity to law and morality. In such situations, a government may feel compelled to subordinate considerations of law and morality to its national interest. In extreme cases, when the very survival of a state is in question, a government may even feel justified in acting beyond the law. In such situations, it is important for the politician or diplomat to have a bad conscience, to be aware of the damage that his action will inflict on the international system, so that the moral values will survive their violation.[10]

If I am neither a Realist nor a Moralist, what am I? If I have to stick a label on myself, I would quote U. Thant and call myself a practical Idealist. I believe that as a Singaporean diplomat, my primary purpose is to protect the independence, sovereignty, territorial integrity and economic well-being of the state of Singapore. I believe that I ought to

---

[10] See Gordon A. Craig and Alexander L. George, *Force and Statecraft, Diplomatic Problems of our Time*, New York, Oxford University Press, 1983, p. 278.

pursue these objectives by means which are lawful and moral. On the rare occasions when the pursuit of my country's vital national interest compels me to do things which are legally or morally dubious, I ought to have a bad conscience and be aware of the damage which I have done to the principle I have violated and to the reputation of my country. I believe that I must always consider the interests of other states and have a decent regard for the opinion of others. I believe that it is in Singapore's long-term interest to strengthen international law and morality, the international system for curbing the use of force and the institutions for the pacific settlement of disputes. Finally, I believe that it is in the interests of all nations to strengthen international co-operation and to make the world's political and economic order more stable, effective and equitable.

Address by Senior Minister Lee Kuan Yew at the 2nd International Institute for Strategic Studies Asia Security Conference, Singapore, Shangri-La Hotel, May 30, 2003

After Iraq

Source: Singapore Government Press Release, Media Relations Division, Ministry of Information, Communications and the Arts, MICA Building, 140 Hill Street, 2nd storey, Singapore 179369.

Introduction

When we met here for the Shangri-La Dialogue in May a year ago, the world faced many threats. Osama bin Laden's al-Qaeda warned the United States of more terror attacks. India and Pakistan had over a million troops facing each other across the line of control in Kashmir. The regime of Saddam Hussein's Iraq continued to flout its disarmament obligations under binding UNSC resolutions.

A year later, although al-Qaeda has hit soft targets elsewhere, its threats to attack the United States and Britain have not materialized. India and Pakistan are restoring air and land links, and war is no longer imminent though a solution to the Kashmir problem is unlikely. The defining event was the removal of Saddam's regime in Iraq after only 21 days of fighting with few casualties.

Earlier in February, Germany, America's most loyal and steadfast European ally for 50 years since the end of the Second World War, joined Russia and France in opposing the US in a public stand-off in the UNSC. It marked the end of an era. When a German Chancellor is closer to a Russian President and at odds with an American President, this is a different world. The French and German leaders would probably have persuaded Chinese President Jiang Zemin to join them if Jiang had not been so focused on China's economic restructuring that requires stable relations with the United States to encourage more trade and investments. China is as strongly against United States unilateralism as France, Germany or Russia. The Chinese describe it as hegemony. But for a long while, China needs equable relations with the United States so that it can grow its economy.

Is this a one-off breach, an accident that both sides can put behind them? Or is it something deeper, more basic? NATO now lacks a common enemy in place of the former Soviet Union. The war in Iraq highlighted this problem. It may have profound geopolitical consequences whose full impact may not be evident for many years. The war shattered the definition of "the West" that for so long was the foundation of global stability during the Cold War. On 23 May, France and Germany supported a new UNSC resolution, giving the US the lead role in administering Iraq. But can trans-Atlantic relations ever return to the previous level of intimacy? This is not just an abstract question because terrorism by Islamic fanatics, the Israel-Palestinian conflict and the shape of the Middle East after Iraq, may sharpen trans-Atlantic differences.

For Americans, after 9/11, the number one enemy is terrorism by Islamic extremists. Many American policy makers believe that the radical Islam of the extremists and the tyranny of Saddam are symptoms of a deeper malaise infecting the Arab world. Some compare the Bush Doctrine of pre-emption of terror to the Truman Doctrine of containment of communism half a century earlier. A recent *NY Times* editorial said: "The end goal is a transformed region in which autocratic governments open the windows to democracy while their moribund societies join the global economy." To achieve this goal, the US has marshalled its enormous power and influence to bear on the Middle East.

Europeans agree that terrorism is a problem, but it's one that Europe has learned to live with: ETA the Basque separatists, the Red Brigade in Germany and the IRA in Britain. They have not suffered a shock like 9/11 and do not feel so vulnerable, in part because since 9/11, Al Qaeda has concentrated its threats on America and Britain. With their long experience in the Middle East, Europeans are also more sceptical about changing the region's basic dynamics.

Europeans regard the primary cause of terrorism as the unending Israeli-Palestinian conflict and America's unqualified support for Israel. They believe that to solve terrorism, this cause must be removed. They find it difficult to refute the Arab view that without unqualified American support and the use of its veto in the UNSC, Israel's policies towards the Palestinians would soon become untenable. Europe is much closer geographically to the Middle East and will suffer directly from any fallout if a war with WMD breaks out across the Mediterranean between Arabs and Israelis. Europeans are also mindful of their own substantial Muslim minorities (13/14 million Muslims in the European Union of whom 4/5 million North Africans are in France alone, and 1.5 million in Britain). They believe that a just and enduring settlement of the Israeli-Palestinian conflict is possible if America not only wills it, but also works in close partnership with a Europe that is seen by the Arabs as more even-handed than the US. Such a settlement will allow Islamic anger to subside and Europe's Muslim problems to become less difficult to manage.

The United States does not agree that the Arab-Israeli conflict is the primary cause of terrorism. It believes that terrorism by Islamic militants has to be considered in the context of the wider problems of the Middle East and the Arab/Muslim world. It sees the need to change the geo-political balance in the Middle East and reshape the political structures of Arab countries to make them more democratic and focused on development and progress.

Washington believes this will allow an Israeli-Palestinian settlement in which all Israel's neighbours, including Lebanon, Syria, Saudi Arabia, the Gulf States and Iraq, will accept Israel's right to exist in something more than the cold peace that now exists between Egypt and Israel. Furthermore, placing the power of the United States right in the heart of the Middle East, in Iraq and the Gulf States, will result in Iran and Syria being flanked by American-friendly states — Iran by Afghanistan to its east and Iraq to its west, and Syria by Israel, Turkey and Iraq. As Colin Powell told Syrian President Bashir Asad, the power equation in the region has changed, and governments in the region have to adjust to the new strategic situation.

Also, Saudi Arabia will no longer be so indispensable to America's strategic interests. America will be in a better position to persuade the Saudis that it would be in their interest to stop the funding and export of Wahhabism. For years, many Saudis and others in the oil-rich Gulf States have bought off their extremists by funding their activities in the world beyond the Arabian Peninsula. The Saudis paid for the building of mosques and madrasahs worldwide and sent ulemas to preach Wahhabism, a severe, fanatical and anti-Western version of Islam. The resulting heightened religiosity has made it easier for Islamic extremists to recruit many Muslims for their jihad of terror. The May 13 suicide bombing in Riyadh and another on May 16 in Casablanca were recent reminders of the dangers of this Saudi policy.

Whether the changes in the Middle East after the fall of Saddam's Iraq can lead to a stable balance in the longer term is not certain. Permanent peaceful co-existence between Arabs and Israelis will be difficult to achieve. A stop to this blood-letting may not dissipate Arab hatred and bitterness against Israelis and Jews. These deep visceral animosities have been socially institutionalized in Palestine and its neighboring Arab countries. Ever since the founding of Israel, Arabs in the Middle East have been taught to hate Israelis and Jews in their schools, madrasahs and mosques, reinforced regularly by repeated media images of powerful Israeli military incursions into the occupied Palestinian territories. After 40 years of patchy economic development, many Arabs feel anger and humiliation that their once glorious Islamic civilization has been diminished by the West, especially America, and corrupted by its licentious culture.

The source of Islamic militancy among Muslims in Southeast Asia has been the increasing fanaticism of extremist Muslims in the Arab world that has been exported by Arab extremists to previously moderate Muslims in Southeast Asia. This Islamic militancy has taken on a life and dynamic of its own. To halt this trend, a peace deal between Israelis and the Palestinians is a necessary but not a sufficient condition. Ending the Palestinian conflict will deprive extremists of a convenient rallying point. But, unless militant groups in the Arab countries and Islamic theocracies are seen to fail, JI and other militant groups in the non-Arab Muslim world will continue to recruit extremists. Even if there is an Israeli-Palestinian settlement, the US and its Western allies must ensure that Islamic militancy is defeated by economic, military and other means to clearly demonstrate to non-Arab Muslims that fanaticism and militancy have no future.

Islamic Extremist Terrorism

Since last year, Jemaah Islamiyah (JI), an affiliate of Al-Qaeda, has committed many acts of terror in the Philippines and Indonesia and one major terrorist act, the bombing in Bali on 12 October 2002, killing 200 Western and Australian tourists. They have paid a price for it. The Indonesian government that hitherto had been neutral *vis-à-vis* Muslim extremists, decided to act. With technical help from the FBI and the Australian Federal special unit, the Indonesian police have arrested the actual perpetrators and their accomplices, some 30 JI operators. But there are hundreds more JI operators still in the region who will regroup and in good time can execute more suicide attacks.

The terrorist jihad is against all non-believers, especially Christians and Jews whether in America, Europe, Pakistan or even Indonesia. Al-Qaeda's leadership has been disrupted and dispersed and they do not appear so far to have restored their ability to execute a spectacular terror attack in the US or UK. So their regional affiliates have blown up Americans and Westerners in Riyadh on 13 May and in Casablanca on 16 May. Other affiliates will attempt similar attacks wherever they can. They will certainly try to attack soft targets in Southeast Asia.

It is in Europe's interest to have America succeed in Iraq. The kind of government and society that emerges in Iraq will have a profound influence on all Arab nations and will have a spill-over effect on non-Arab Muslims. The present disorder delays the rebuilding of Iraq's political structures. However, the possibility of a more fundamentalist Iraq is real; Iraqi Shias form 60 percent of the population. They are well-organized around their Imams in their respective mosques and the influence of the principal imams, or ayahtollahs, is considerable.

Therefore, free voting for a representative government can produce a more Islamic government in Iraq.

East Asia and North Korea

After the demonstration of American technological military wizardry in Iraq, is it more likely that there could be less blackmailing by the North Koreans in their talks with the Americans? I believe, despite all the bluster, the North knows that there are limits to brinksmanship when blackmailing a Bush Presidency.

Beijing wants North Korea intact. An imploded North Korea and reunification will bring American troops up to the Yalu River. A nuclear North Korea is not in China's interest because Japan would then have to go nuclear. So China will have to take a stand against a nuclear North Korea.

The South Korean President Roh Moo Hyun was elected at the end of last year on an anti-American platform. The South does not want an imploded North that would be a huge burden. Peaceful reunification in the very long term is the desired outcome. Should the North have nuclear bombs, the South would then inherit them. After President Roh's meeting with President Bush, US and South Korean positions towards the North no longer seem to be so much at odds.

Japan does not want a North Korea that can threaten it with missiles and nuclear warheads. An imploded North Korea may land Japan with some refugees, but it will not be in the numbers that will flee into South Korea and China. A reunited Korea is not necessarily good for Japan.

For America, the simplest solution is an imploded North, and it does not matter if reunification is the result. If a peaceful resolution to the present impasse requires yielding to Pyongyang's blackmail for aid and a promise of non-aggression, that will stick in the throats of the Americans. In any case, the North is unlikely to give up its nuclear weapons whatever the deal.

Because the four parties most closely involved with North Korea — United States, South Korea, Japan, China — have different objectives, a neat solution is not obvious.

Conclusion

To conclude, British Prime Minister Tony Blair wants Europe to embrace the United States as a full partner and as such, influence the direction and policy of the United States. France, on the other hand, believes that Europe should be a counterweight to restrain American excessive unilateralism.

Europeans were naturally pro-American since the end of World War II, when the Marshall plan salvaged them from the ravages of the war and NATO protected them from Soviet domination. More recently, some Europeans, besides the French, have become uncomfortable when they see the US, confident of its technological supremacy, pursue what they feel are high-risk solutions to complex problems. Up to the present, Blair's policy of supporting the United States and influencing its decisions as a partner can claim to work. But if America does not cultivate its friends and allies with more tender loving care, coalitions of the willing may become smaller.

Throughout history, every force has generated a counterforce. For the present, Russia, China and many countries in the European Union want to maintain good or friendly relations with the United States. There is reason to hope that tending to these relations can prolong US pre-eminence. Not to do so may persuade more nations that the way to restrain American unilateralism is to join a group of all those opposed to it.

Keynote Speech by Minister Mentor Lee Kuan Yew at the Official Opening of the Lee Kuan Yew School of Public Policy, Singapore, Shangri-La Hotel, April 4, 2005

Managing Globalization: Lessons from China and India

Source: Singapore Government Press Release, Media Relations Division, Ministry of Information, Communications and the Arts, MICA Building, 140 Hill Street, 2nd storey, Singapore 179369.

Introduction

Renaissance spreads in Asia

An enormous transformation is underway in Asia. Across the region, countries are reforming their methods of governance and the way they decide public policies. They want to catch up and prosper with the rest of the developed world.

The original four Asian Tigers — Hong Kong, Taiwan, South Korea and Singapore — followed Japan. They led the pack, followed by Malaysia, Thailand and Indonesia. The Japanese called this the "flying geese" pattern of economic development, with each new follower gaining technology from the leader and passing it on eventually to the next group of followers. But this formation of countries is not large enough to move the world.

China and India will shake the world. Together, they are home to 40 percent of the world's population. Both are among the world's fastest-growing economies: China, 8–10 percent; India, 6–7 percent. China is the factory of the world; India the outsourcing service center, first in call centers and now moving to more sophisticated business process operations and clinical research activities of global corporations.

The Chinese and Indians are learning not just from Japan and the Asian NIEs, but from the advanced countries. They are selectively adopting and adapting different models and principles of governance to propel them into the front ranks. In some industries, they have already leapfrogged the rest of Asia. The outcome will be a major rebalancing of the world.

Origins of the Lee Kuan Yew School of Public Policy

The Lee Kuan Yew School of Public Policy started in 1992 as a small Public Policy Program in the National University of Singapore. Its aim was to study the different systems of governance in our immediate region and to offer public officials from the region a rigorous training on the best practices to implement sound public policies.

With China's and India's rise, the new School will expand its research and teaching to include these two largest countries in the world. They provide a rich field of research and may yield clues on why some are more successful in catching up with the advanced economies. Is it a matter of importing particular systems and policies? Or are there deeper factors that have not been studied?

Evolution of my views on China and India

I have taken a deep interest in both China and India ever since I started my political life in 1950. Like all democratic socialists of the

1950s, I have tried to analyze and forecast which giant would make the grade. I had hoped it would be democratic India, not communist China.

By the 1980s, I had become more realistic and accepted the differences between the two. It is simplistic to believe that democracy and free markets are the formula that must lead to progress and wealth. However, I am convinced the contrary axiom is true that central planning and state-owned or nationalized enterprises lead to inefficiency and poor returns, whether the government is authoritarian or democratic. Moreover, even if China and India were both democratic, or authoritarian or communist, their performance would be different. I now believe that, besides the standard economic yardsticks for productivity and competitiveness, there are intangible factors like culture, religion and other ethnic characteristics and national ethos that affect the outcome.

At the start after World War II, China was behind India. China's infrastructure and population were devastated by the Japanese occupation from 1937–1945. Then a civil war followed. After the Communist victory in 1949, China adopted the system of governance and economic policies of the Soviet Union.

At independence in August 1947, India had ample sterling balances, a good system of governance and many top-class institutions. It had functioning institutions for a democracy, the rule of law, a neutral highly-trained civil service, defence force and proficiency in the English language.

The situation deteriorated over time. India adopted central planning with results nearly as damaging as those of China. India's political leaders are determined to reform, but the Indian bureaucracy has been slower and resistant to change. Regional jostling and corruption do not help. Furthermore, populist democracy makes Indian policies less consistent, with regular changes in ruling parties. For example, Hangzhou and Bangalore are comparable cities. Hangzhou's new airport opened in 2000; Bangalore's has been on the drawing board for years and was only given the go-ahead by the state government in December 2004.

China, the economically more backward country in 1950, caught up with India and has now surpassed India in several sectors. How did communist China catch up, and why did democratic India lose its lead?

Comparison of the Chinese and Indian public sector

Did China pull ahead because it had better systems of governance and methods of determining public policies?

Tax system. Ten years ago, China had a complicated tax system. There were provincial and municipal sales taxes, provincial border taxes, excise duties and levies. By imposing a single Value Added Tax on manufactured goods, China has made tax collection efficient and effective.

India has made several unsuccessful attempts to introduce a national VAT, the last on 1 April 2005 when 20 states switched to VAT, but eight are still holding out.

Corruption bedevils both, but bureaucratic red tape has lowered India's efficiency and effectiveness more than China's. It takes 88 days to secure all the permits needed to start a business in India, compared to 46 in China. Insolvency procedures take 11 years, as against 2.6 in China. In spite of the disasters of the Great Leap Forward in 1958 and the Cultural Revolution during 1966–1976, China pulled itself up after its open door policy from 1978.

Comparison of the Chinese and Indian private sector

On the other hand, India's private sector is superior to China's. Indian companies, although not on par with the best American or Japanese companies because of India's semi-closed market, nevertheless include several near world-class companies, like Tata Consultancy Services, Infosys and Wipro. Indian multinationals are now acquiring western companies in their home markets. Moreover, Indian companies follow international rules of corporate governance and offer higher return-on-equity as against Chinese companies. And India has transparent and functioning capital markets.

China has not yet created great companies, despite being the third-largest spender in the world on R&D. Also, Chinese corporate fraud is on a much larger scale.

Singapore — More economic interaction with China than with India

Singapore has more exposure to China's governance and public policies than India's. For 10 years, Singapore trained nearly 1,000 officials from Suzhou to plan, manage and develop an integrated township called the Suzhou Industrial Park. We trained them in various disciplines with the emphasis on the planning and management of an integrated city with industry, services, commerce, private and public housing, public utilities, schools, hospitals, parks, golf courses and recreational areas, sited all to be in 70 sq km. There were many difficult problems in the early years because of our different mindsets, although we share similar, but not identical, language and culture. However, despite the travail, after 10 years the results are startling.

They have not only learned about the specific areas in which we instructed them, but they have observed how we have cleaned up Singapore and its waterways, greened it, planned, built and managed our public housing and town planning.

In 1994, Suzhou was dilapidated, canals stagnant and fetid, shorn of its charm as the "Venice of China". Now, they have flushed the canals and greened up their banks. Boutique restaurants, hotels, shopping malls and all the attractiveness of a well-lived modern city that preserved their old buildings, spruced up and refurbished. They studied what we have done in Singapore. What we took 40 years to do they were able to adopt, adapt and implement in 10 years.

Over a thousand Chinese officials, selected by different centers, the Communist Party's Central Organization Department, the Central Party School and the China Association of Mayors, have been studying Singapore's system, its economic and social development, public administration, anti-corruption practices, financial management, human resource development, social security and taxation system, urban planning, management and social development. Several of them have taken Master's degrees at NUS and NTU in Public Management, Public Policy and Business Administration and Managerial Economics.

They have selectively incorporated and bud-grafted specific policies they find useful. In several Chinese cities where Singapore's Housing and Development Board has done public housing projects, they have been able to replicate these townships with improved designs for the flats to suit their different climatic conditions. The speed at which they have learned has no parallel anywhere else.

In India, Singapore's EDB and a JTC-led consortium invested in the International Technology Park of Bangalore (ITBP). It is a self-contained oasis, with independent power supply. The Park has become an icon showcasing India's accommodation of MNCs. The Indians have duplicated such "oases" in other cities, including the Hi-tech Park in Hyderabad and Tidel Park in Chennai. But the rate of replication appears slower than in China. Could it be bureaucratic inertia? Or are Indian private enterprises and consumers slower than the Chinese in the diffusion of technology and innovation, from one player to the next and one industry to another? Why are mobile phone penetration rates in China higher than in India? This School should study this phenomenon.

China and India: Studying and Learning from Each Other

Thickening ties

The Chinese and Indians realize they have much to learn from one another. China and India are going to assiduously study each other's experiences, and try to acquire the strong points of the other. They will spur each other to excel.

What both must avoid is to be placed in opposing camps, one with the US and the other against.

What can China and India learn from each other?

The Chinese are learning English with great enthusiasm. They may catch up with India, even though they may never have that layer at the top, like the Indians do, who are steeped in the English language and its literature. But the Chinese will have enough English to network easily with businessmen and scholars in America and Europe. In technical and technological skills, China is following India's lead and has started to supply software engineers to multinational corporations like Cisco.

India has grown quite rapidly over the last decade with far lower investment rates than China. China must learn to be as efficient as India in utilizing its resources.

The Chinese are keen to develop a services sector like India's. For example, they have contracted an Indian company to train 1,000 Chinese software project managers from Shenzhen in etiquette, communications and negotiations skills. Huawei, a leading Chinese technology company, invested in Bangalore to tap its software skills. The Chinese want to attain international standards for the software outsourcing industry and learn how to deal with US and European clients as India is doing.

India wants to be as successful as China in attracting foreign and domestic investments in manufacturing. India must emulate the effective way in which China has built up its extensive communications and transportation infrastructure, power plants and water resources, and implement policies that lead to huge FDI in manufacturing, high job creation and high growth. India's spectacular growth has been in IT services, which do not generate high job creation. But it has now drawn up a massive highway construction program that is more than half completed.

Challenges facing China and India

China and India have their specific advantages, but also face similar challenging social, economic and political problems. China has to restructure its state-owned enterprises, fix its weak banking sector and ensure its economy continues to grow fast enough to absorb the still huge army of unemployed. India has poor infrastructure, high administrative and regulatory barriers to business, and large fiscal deficits, especially at the state level, that are a drag on investment and job creation.

In fifty years, China and the rest of Northeast Asia (Japan, Korea, Taiwan) will be at the high-end of the technology ladder, Southeast

Asia mainly at the lower and middle-end of the value-added ladder where there will still be large opportunities for efficient competitors. On the other hand, India will have certain regions at the high-end of the technology ladder, but it may have vast rural areas lagging behind, like the Russian hinterland during the Soviet era. To avoid this, India has to build up its infrastructure of expressway across the subcontinent, faster and more railway connections, more airports, expand telecoms and open up its rural areas.

Why are the Chinese ahead?

The Chinese are more homogeneous: 90% Han; one language and culture; one written script, with varying pronunciations. Having shared a common destiny over several millennia, they are more united as a people. And they can swiftly mobilize resources across the continent for their tasks.

China's Deng Xiaoping started his open door policy in 1978. In the 28 years since, China has more than tripled its per capita GDP, and the momentum of its reforms has transformed the lives of its people, thus making its market reform policies irreversible.

India's one billion people are of different ethnic groups with different languages, cultures and traditions. It recognizes 18 main languages and 844 dialects and six main religions. India has to make continuous and great efforts to hold together different peoples who were brought together in the last two centuries into one polity by the British Raj that joined parts of the Mogul empire with the princely states in the Hindi-speaking north and the Tamil, Telegu and other linguistic/racial groups in the south.

India began liberalizing in 1990, and then in fits and starts. However, India's system of democracy and rule of law gives it a long-term advantage over China, although in the early phases China has the advantage of faster implementation of its reforms. As China develops and becomes a largely urban society, its political system must evolve to accommodate a large, better educated middle-class that will be highly educated, better informed and connected with the outside world, one that expects higher quality of life in a clean environment, and wants to have its views heard by a government that is transparent and free from corruption.

China and India are to launch FTA negotiations that may be completed in a few years. I understand Premier Wen Jiabao will be visiting India soon, followed by President Hu Jintao shortly afterwards. Their closer economic ties will have a huge impact on the world. ASEAN and Singapore can only benefit from their closer economic links. Many Indians are in influential positions in Wall Street, in US MNCs, World Bank, IMF and research institutes and universities. This network will give India an extra edge. More Chinese are joining this American-based international network, but they do not yet have the same facility in the English language and culture. And because of Sino-US rivalry, there will be greater reserve when Americans interact with them.

For a modern economy to succeed, a whole population must be educated. The Chinese have developed their human capital more effectively through a nationalized education system. In 1999, 98% of Chinese children have completed 5 years of primary education as against 53% of Indian children. India did not have universal education and educational standards diverge much more sharply than in China. In some states like Kerala, participation in primary schools is 90%. In some states it is less than 30%. Overall, in 2001, India's illiteracy rate was 42%, against China's 14%.

India had many first-rate universities at independence. Except for a few top universities such as the Indian Institute of Technology and Indian Institute of Management that still rank with the best, it could not maintain the high standards of its many other universities. Political pressures made for quotas for admission based on caste or connections with MPs. China has repaired the damage the Cultural Revolution inflicted on their universities. Admission to Chinese universities is based on the entrance examination.

China has built much better physical infrastructure. China has 30,000 km of expressway, ten times as much as India, and six times as many mobile and fixed-line telephones per 1,000 persons. To catch up, India would have to invest massively in its roads, airports, seaports, telecommunications and power networks. The current Indian government has recognized this in its budget. It must implement the projects expeditiously.

The Chinese bureaucracy has been methodical in adopting best practices in their system of governance and public policies. They have studied and are replicating what Japan, Korea, Taiwan, Singapore and Hong Kong have done. China's coastal cities are catching up fast. But China's vast rural interior is lagging behind, exposing serious disparities in wealth and job opportunities. The central government is acutely aware of these dangers and have despatched some of the most energetic and successful mayors and provincial governors to these disadvantaged provinces to narrow the gap.

China's response to these looming problems is proactive and multifaceted. For example, to meet energy needs, China National Petroleum Corporation and China National Offshore Oil Corporation (CNOOC) have moved into Indonesian oil and gas fields. Chinese companies have even gone to Venezuela, Angola and Sudan.

India signed a recent agreement with Myanmar to import gas by pipeline via Bangladesh. The Indian government plans to consolidate their state-owned oil companies and act proactively like China's CNOOC. The ASEAN-China Free Trade Agreement is an example of China's pre-emptive moves. China moved faster than Japan by opening up its agricultural sector to ASEAN countries. India is also negotiating a Closer Economic Cooperation Agreement with ASEAN, but China has gotten there first.

Caveat

The *Financial Times*, 29 March 2005, wrote: "The lack of a robust capital market is likely to have a strong influence on the future shape and development of Chinese capitalism. Cheap manufacturing might be China's current competitive advantage but, in the long run, Beijing planners want the country to move more into lucrative high-technology sectors that provide better-paying jobs. China will need a dynamic private sector, run by entrepreneurs who have the drive to build innovative companies. Yet it is exactly these sorts of companies that are being squeezed out by an equity market that caters mostly to state-controlled groups. Private-sector companies can get bank financing, especially if they have good political connections. Yet the lack of an equity funding route is likely to curtail China's ability to develop a strong private sector. In this area, many argue that India is already ahead, as most of its biggest companies come from the private sector and have grown through raising capital on the equity and bond markets. China needs a robust stock market to stave off a looming pensions crisis. One of the by-products of the one-child policy introduced 25 years ago is that in a decade or so many more people will be retiring than entering the workforce." This is China's big negative, its rapidly aging population as a result of its severe one-child family policy. There is no precedent for a country to grow old before it has grown rich. India — average age, 26, compared to China's 33 and still with much faster population growth — will enjoy a bigger demographic dividend, but it would have to educate its people better, or else the opportunity will turn into a burden.

What Can the Lee Kuan Yew School of Public Policy Offer?

The School as a neutral venue

China and India will compete with one another and with the rest of the developed world. Their systems of governance and the way they arrive at and implement public policies will be major factors in their performance.

The Lee Kuan Yew School of Public Policy, based in Singapore, can offer China, India, the region and the world, a neutral venue for scholars and public officials to gather, discuss and understand why a society succeeds. In this neutral venue, scholars will be free to objectively compare and contrast the different systems that exist and assess what have made for better outcomes.

And they can also determine the extent to which non-measurable factors like culture, religion and language affect the final outcome.

Although Singapore has had broad interaction with both China and India in the last 20 years, our ties with India go back to the time Singapore was founded by the British Raj. Singapore was governed in 1819 from Calcutta. We also have strong links with the United States,

Britain and Europe. The renaissance of China and India in economic, social and cultural fields will shift the world's center of gravity from the Atlantic to the Pacific and Indian Oceans.

Historically, these two great countries have influenced the economies, religions and cultures of Southeast Asia. Hence the name Indo-Chinese peninsula and its mix of Indian and Chinese culture. The region also has the largest number of Muslims in the world. The Islamic world is in turbulent flux. The outcome in the region will be influenced by developments in the Middle East, China and India. Southeast Asia is for the first time simultaneously influenced by the Christian West, Islam, China and India.

Southeast Asian countries have inherited different systems of government from their colonial powers — Indonesia from the Dutch; Vietnam, Laos and Cambodia from the French; Malaysia, Singapore and Brunei from the British. Myanmar lost its British legacy when the Japanese army occupied the country. Thailand, never a colony, has evolved its own system. I believe the British instituted the best system benefiting Singapore, Malaysia and Brunei. There is no reason why Indonesia, Vietnam and the other countries cannot adopt the best practices of the successful nations. Indeed, Singapore, Malaysia and Brunei have updated the system they inherited by incorporating better practices from other countries.

For over a decade, the Public Policy Program has brought together senior officials from all over the region to study the best practices of governance and policymaking. The diverse student mix has helped the diffusion of ideas and practices. Officials have been able to compare notes and learn from one another. The professors have provided consulting services to governments in the region on how to improve their public policies and systems of governance. The School can provide a blend of theory and practice. One of the School's professors is now acting as a WHO consultant to implement performance-based budgeting in government hospitals in Philippines. This idea was proposed by a group of Filipinos who had studied Singapore's healthcare financing system while attending the former Public Policy Program. When the School's focus includes China and India, there will be more such value-added outcomes. This School is the venue for scholars, officials and students from the world over, especially from China and India, to gather, research, and exchange ideas on how societies are best governed in a globalizing world. All participants will benefit from a rigorous study of policies that have succeeded and those that failed.

Beyond China, India and Southeast Asia

To increase our understanding of the systems of governance that work and can improve the lives of people, we must compare European and US patterns of governance and public policy formulation with those of China, India and Southeast Asia.

Singapore's own experiences with governance and public policies may illuminate some of the key factors that made for its successful development by borrowing and modifying policies and ideas from Europe and America.

All said and done, it is the creativity of leadership, its willingness to learn from experience elsewhere, to implement good ideas quickly and decisively through an efficient public service, and to convince the majority of people that tough reforms are worth taking, that decides a country's development and progress. Whether China or India will prove to be the better model for other developing countries, we will know by the middle of this century.

Speech by Minister Mentor Lee Kuan Yew at the 37th Jawaharlal Nehru Memorial Lecture, New Delhi, November 21, 2005

India in an Asian Renaissance

Source: Singapore Government Press Release, Media Relations Division, Ministry of Information, Communications and the Arts, MICA Building, 140 Hill Street, 2nd storey, Singapore 179369.

I thank the Prime Minister Manmohan Singh and the Jawaharlal Nehru Memorial Fund, Mrs Sonia Gandhi (its Chair Person) for inviting me to give the Nehru Lecture.

I belong to that generation of Asian nationalists who looked up to India's freedom struggle and its leaders, Mahatma Gandhi and Pandit Jawaharlal Nehru.

I had read Nehru's books like The Discovery of India, culled from his letters from prison to his daughter Indira and many of his speeches. On 14 August 1947, when I was a young student in Cambridge, I remember vividly the moving and unforgettable opening of Nehru's broadcast on the eve of independence: "Long years ago we made a tryst with destiny, and now the time comes when we shall redeem our pledge, not wholly or in full measure, but very substantially. At the stroke of the midnight hour, when the world sleeps, India will awake to life and freedom. A moment comes, which comes but rarely in history, when we step out from the old to the new, when an age ends, and when the soul of a nation, long suppressed, finds utterance."

The destiny Nehru envisaged was of a modern, industrialized, democratic and secular India that would take its place in the larger historic flows of the second half of the 20th century.

Nehru never doubted India's place in the world. When imprisoned in Ahmadnager Fort during the Second World War, he wrote:

> *Though not directly a Pacific state, India will inevitably exercise an important influence there. . . . Her position gives an economic and strategic importance in a part of the world which is going to develop rapidly in the future.*

Nehru's speeches resonated with me. I shared intellectual and emotional roots with Nehru because I had also experienced discrimination and subjugation under the British Raj and admired Nehru for his vision of a secular multiracial India, a country that does not discriminate between citizens because of their race, language, religion or culture. I first visited New Delhi in 1959 for a conference of the International Commission of Jurists (ICJ). Nehru opened the conference at the Vigyan Bhavan. He arrived in a modest Hindustan (Morris Oxford, Made in India). Later in April 1962, when I was Prime Minister of Singapore, Nehru gave me time for several discussions about Singapore's merger with Malaya to form the Federation of Malaysia. He encouraged and supported my ideas. Nehru received me again in February 1964 on my return from a visit to 17 countries in Africa.

Like Nehru, I had been influenced by the ideas of the British Fabian society. But I soon realized that before distributing the pie, I first had to bake it. So I departed from welfarism because it sapped at people's self-reliance and their desire to excel and succeed. I also abandoned the model of industrialization through import substitution. When most of the Third World was deeply suspicious of exploitation by western MNCs (multinational corporations), Singapore invited them in. They helped us grow, brought in technology and knowhow, and raised productivity levels faster than any alternative strategy could.

Nehru had a great vision for India and for Asia, and his elegant style of writing and speech captivated many young minds in the

British empire. He had insights into the causes of India's problems, but, burdened by too many issues, he left the implementation of his ideas and policies to his ministers and secretaries. Sadly, they did not achieve the results India deserved.

Nehru's ideal of democratic socialism was bureaucratized by Indian officials who were influenced by the Soviet model of central planning. That eventually led to the "Licence Raj", corruption and slow growth.

The end of the Cold War and the collapse of the Soviet Union undercut the strategic premises of India's external and economic policies. By 1991, with the country on the verge of bankruptcy, India had no choice but to change. Some Indians believe that, had Rajiv Gandhi lived to serve a second term as India's Prime Minister, he would have pushed for major reform. But he was cut down before he was able to.

It was left to PM Narasimha Rao to make the big move in 1991. Later that year, then Finance Minister Manmohan Singh and Commerce Minister Chidambaram gave a seminar in Singapore on India's new policy of reform and opening up. In 1992, Prime Minister Narasimha Rao met Singapore's then Prime Minister Goh Chok Tong at the Non-Aligned Conference in Jakarta and persuaded him to visit India with a delegation of Singapore businessmen. PM Goh visited India from 23-30 January 1994 and returned enthused.

In January 1996, I visited New Delhi and spoke to civil servants and businessmen on the changes that Prime Minister Rao and his team were putting into place. I said that India's "tryst with destiny" had been repeatedly postponed.

When I published the second volume of my Memoirs in 2000, I wrote, "India is a nation of unfulfilled greatness. Its potential has lain fallow, under-used."

Time to Keep the Tryst

I am happy to now revise my view. Nehru's view of India's place in the world and of India as a global player is within India's grasp.

Since 1991, India has changed governments from Congress to BJP to Janata Dal to BJP, and back again to Congress. There have been six

Prime Ministers. The pace of reforms has varied, but there has been no change in basic direction. The middle class has expanded. There is now no stigma in acquiring wealth. Indians have seen what market-orientated policies have done for China and they do not want to be left behind.

The rise of India and China is changing the global balance. Together, they account for about 40 percent of the world's working-age population and 19 percent of the global economy in PPP (purchasing power parity) terms. On present trends, in 20 years, their collective share of the global economy will match their percentage of the global population, which is roughly where they were in the 18th century, before European colonialism engulfed them. China's and India's trade, investments and other economic relations with the countries of East Asia and the Pacific are reshaping Asia's economic geography. India is an important ASEAN Dialogue Partner, a member of the ASEAN Regional Forum, and an inaugural member of the East Asia Summit this December. And there is no reason why it should not join APEC (Asia-Pacific Economic Cooperation) after it has developed a thick web of economic ties across the Pacific.

East Asia is coalescing, brought together by market forces. India, China and Japan are readjusting their relationships with each other and with the US. This will not be an easy process because all countries want to preserve their independence and space to grow. If there are no mishaps by 2050, the US, China, India and Japan will be economic heavyweights, as will Russia if it converts its revenue from oil and gas into long-term value in infrastructure and non-oil industries.

India is an intrinsic part of this unfolding new world order. India can no longer be dismissed as a "*wounded civilisation*", in the hurtful phrase of a westernized non-resident Indian author (V.S. Naipal). Instead, the western media, market analysts and international financial institutions now showcase India as a success story and the next big opportunity.

This is a comforting development for the US and the West, that a multi-party India is able to take off and keep pace with single-party China.

Forbes Asia recently reported that US venture firms will raise US$1 billion for India by the end of this year. India has emerged as a major power in the IT sector. It is the largest call center in the world. Almost half of the largest global corporates now do at least some of their back office work in India. Indian R&D centers of American technology firms are reported to file more patents than Bell Labs. This year, India announced more than 1,300 applications for drug patents, second only to the US and 25 percent more than Germany, way ahead of the UK and Japan.

The US is now courting a nuclear India as a strategic partner. The EU has also launched a strategic partnership with India, and Japan wants a global partnership with India. These are indices of India's growing weight in the world. Many countries, including Singapore, supported India's bid to be a Permanent Member of the UN Security Council. Nehru's vision is within grasp and India's leaders must realize it in the next few decades.

China and India

I have always taken a keen interest in both China and India. Like all democratic socialists of the 1950s, I tried to forecast which giant would make the higher grade. I had rather hoped it would be a democratic India. By the 1980s, however, I accepted that each had its strengths and weaknesses and that the final outcome would depend on their economic policies, the execution of those policies, the responsiveness of the government to the needs of the people, and most of all, the nature of the culture of the two civilizations.

Whether Asia will take its place in the world as Nehru wanted depends on how both India and China work together as they rise and actively set out to avoid ending up in opposing camps. It is vital that they understand where they stand *vis-à-vis* one another. They must not be paranoid and suspicious of each other in a game of one-upmanship. Instead they can cooperate and compete economically, and each improve its performance by using the other's progress as benchmarks for what they should do better. India's bilateral relations with China have improved significantly in recent years after both sides decided to resolve long outstanding issues.

Compare and Contrast: India and China

The world is fascinated by the renaissance of Asia's two largest and most ancient civilizations, and political and business leaders compare and contrast their progress and prospects.

At independence in 1947, two years before the Chinese Communist Party liberated China, India was ahead in many sectors. Both lost steam by adopting the planned economy. But because of its "Great Leap Forward" and "Cultural Revolution", China suffered more. However, Deng Xiaoping was able to acknowledge China's mistakes and China's course dramatically changed when he returned to power in 1978.

India has superior private sector companies. China has the more efficient and decisive administrative system. China has invested heavily in infrastructure. India's underinvested infrastructure is woefully inadequate. India has a stronger banking system and capital markets than China. India has stronger institutions, in particular, a well-developed legal system which should provide a better environment for the creation and protection of Intellectual Property. But a judicial backlog of an estimated 26 million cases drags down the system. One former Indian Chief Justice of India's Supreme Court has given a legal opinion in a foreign court that India's judicial system was practically non-functional in settling commercial disputes.

Both India and China have excellent universities, at the peak of their systems. India's institutes of technology and management are world class. China is determined to upgrade its top 10 universities to world class status. Overall, China's education system is more comprehensive. China's illiteracy rate is below 10%, India's about 40%. India's narrower band of educated people will be a weakness in the longer-term. And although top quality Indian manpower is in high demand, large numbers of engineers and graduates lack the skills required in a changing economy and remain unemployed. However, India has a larger English-speaking elite than China. But only over half of each Indian cohort completes primary school — a big loss.

After liberalization, China and India have followed different models of development, maximizing their respective strengths. China adopted the standard East Asian model, emphasizing export-oriented manufacturing. China has been immensely more successful in attracting FDI. India has focused on IT and knowledge-based services. Job creation is much slower in India and will continue to remain so until India's infrastructure is brought up to date to attract the many manufacturers who will come to use India's low cost workers and efficient services.

China's GDP for manufacturing is 52%, India's 27%; in agriculture China's is 15%, India's 22%; for services China's 33%, India's 51%. Over the last decade, in the service sector, India has averaged 7.6% annual growth, China 8.8%; in manufacturing, India's growth is 5.7%, China's 12.8%.

India and China should cooperate and compete with each other, spurring one another to greater heights. ASEAN will be a major beneficiary. As Senior Minister Goh Chok Tong once said, India and China can be the two wings of the jumbo jet for Southeast Asia.

India should benchmark itself not just against its own past, but against the best in Asia. India can take heart from the achievements and performance of Non-Resident Indians (NRI) in free market economies such as the US, UK and even Singapore, where large numbers of NRIs have assumed high corporate positions in multinational corporations.

Both India and China have done much better than most of the world. In the decade from 1994 to 2004, India's GDP grew two-fold from US$310 billion to US$661 billion. But during the same period, China's GDP grew three-fold from US$542 billion to US$1,649 billion. In 1984, India's GDP was about 30% smaller than China's. A decade later, it was more than 40% smaller and by 2004 it was about 60% smaller. Such a wide disparity is unnecessary. India can and should narrow the gap by embarking on a new round of reforms.

Walking on Two Legs

Can India keep pace with China's growth? Yes, if India does more in those sectors where China has done better.

The Chinese are learning English with great enthusiasm, and are keen to develop a services sector like India's. All the leading Indian

IT players are expanding in China, and training thousands of Chinese software programmers. One Indian company, Zensar Technologies Ltd, has been contracted to train 1,000 Chinese software project managers from Shenzhen in etiquette, communication and negotiation skills. Huawei, a leading Chinese technology company, has invested in Bangalore to tap its software skills. The Chinese want to reach international standards for the software outsourcing industry. They are not too proud to learn from India. In Dalian, Singapore is helping to develop an IT park which will be specifically marketed to Indian software companies interested in the Northeast Asian market.

But India cannot grow into a major economy on services alone. Since the industrial revolution, no country has become a major economy without becoming an industrial power.

Just as China is learning from India to improve its performance in the IT sector, so India must emulate China's success in attracting FDI and the jobs they create in manufacturing. It can do this by building infrastructure and educating and raising the skill levels of its workers.

Arvind Panagariya, a professor of Indian political economy at Columbia University, USA, puts the issue clearly. He noted that some have argued that India can focus on IT, grow rapidly in services, skip industrialization, and yet transform itself from a primarily rural and agricultural country into a modern economy. He dismissed such ideas as "*hopelessly flawed*" and "*far-fetched*".

IT is less than 2% of India's GDP. While services have grown rapidly, the bulk of the growth is from service sectors where wages and productivity are low. Business services, which include software and IT-enabled services, account for only 0.3% of GDP. Only manufacturing can mop up India's vast pool of unemployed, narrow the urban-rural divide and reduce poverty. Professor Panagariya concluded:

The right strategy for India is to walk on two legs: traditional labor intensive industry and modern IT. Both legs need strengthening through further reforms ....

India's relatively young population can be an asset if they are universally well-educated. UN forecasts that India's population will outstrip China's by 2030. Job creation through faster GDP growth is therefore an urgent necessity. Growth in IT and other services will not create enough jobs. IT-related jobs make up only one-quarter of one percent of India's labor force.

To create jobs, the main thrust of reforms must be in manufacturing. That requires a change in labor laws to allow employers to retrench workers when business demand is down, streamlining the judicial processes, reducing the fiscal deficit, loosening up the bureaucracy, and most of all, improving infrastructure. Let me focus on the last two as I believe they are crucial and inter-connected.

Industrialization cannot take off without adequate infrastructure: better roads, and a reliable supply of power and clean water, better ports and airports. By one estimate, economic losses from congestion and poor roads alone are as high as US$4–6 billion a year. Another estimate is that the cost of most infrastructure services in India is about 50% to 100% higher than in China. The average cost of electricity for manufacturing in India is about double that in China; railway transport costs in India are three times those in China. China has spent over eight times as much as India on its infrastructure. Three years ago, China's total capital spending on electricity, construction, transportation, telecommunications and real estate was US$260 billion or more than 20 percent of its GDP as compared to US$31 billion or 8 percent of India's GDP.

If there are budgetary constraints, the answer is to privatize these infrastructure projects. There are well-established construction companies, Japanese, Korean and others, that have done many such infrastructure projects on franchise terms.

One area where India has done well is its telecommunications infrastructure. This has been a critical factor for India's IT success. India needs to aggressively privatize infrastructure development and open it to foreign investment. Then, FDI flows will increase. And the bureaucracy must not impose onerous conditions that will hamper this privatization.

The Political and Economic Risk Consultancy (PERC) based in Hong Kong, recently surveyed expatriate businessmen on bureaucracy and red tape in Asia. India was rated worst out of the 12 countries covered. PERC's conclusion was that:

> *The Government would like to liberalize many sectors, and there are plenty of announcements of new initiatives to do so. But when push comes to shove, bureaucratic inertia has been extremely difficult to overcome.*

The World Bank has also done its own study. It found that in India, it can take a decade to close a business through insolvency proceedings. It also found, among other things, that official fees amount to almost 13 percent of a property transaction in India as against just over 3 percent in China.

My secretaries asked Singapore businessmen with investments in India what, apart from infrastructure, they found as major constraints. To a man, they replied it was the bureaucracy.

They believe it is a mindset problem. The average Indian civil servant still sees himself primarily as a regulator and not as a facilitator. The average Indian bureaucrat has not yet accepted that it is not a sin to make profits and become rich. The average Indian bureaucrat has little trust in India's business community. They view Indian businessmen as money grabbing opportunists who do not have the welfare of the country at heart; and all the more so if they are foreign businessmen. Deng Xiaoping said at the start of China's open door policy, it was glorious to be rich. The sequel is reported in *Forbes Asia*, 14 November 2005, where it listed over 300 of China's richest, 40 of them with thumbnail CVs in a centre-fold. All are new entrepreneurs creating jobs and spreading wealth. Now, after private enterprise and the free market have generated wealth in the coastal provinces, China's leaders have concentrated on spreading growth to the inland provinces by building infrastructure and offering generous economic incentives for investments.

One Singapore businessman told me this story. He entertained a former senior Indian civil servant to lunch in Singapore. Some months later, when he was in India, the former civil servant reciprocated by hosting a dinner at which several other guests were present. His host made this surprising comment that he was amazed to see that in Singapore, a business could be successful without being dishonest.

India must find some way to reward bureaucrats who facilitate, not hinder, investments and enterprise, whether Indian or foreign.

A factor worth noting: India gets a much better economic return for the investment it makes in its economy because India's private sector capital efficiency is high. If India opens up fully to FDI, the results will be profitable for the investor and add considerable employment and added GDP growth for India. With jobs, there will be a trickle-down of wealth to millions of Indian workers, as there has been in East Asia.

Politics is the Issue

What India has achieved since 1991 should not be underrated. There have been many successes. The Delhi Metro is one. Bharat Forge, the largest Indian exporter of auto components and the leading global chassis component manufacturer, is another example in the manufacturing sector. There are others. The question is why are there not many more of them?

There is no dearth of excellent analyses by Indians about this problem. An entire library could be assembled on the subject. I consulted two books: *The Future of India* by Bimal Jalan, who was Governor of the Reserve Bank of India from 1997 to 2003, Chairman of the Economic Advisory Council to the Prime Minister and has represented India at the IMF and World Bank; and one other book, *Governance* by Arun Shourie, who has held several government portfolios and is a well-known writer. To sum up their arguments for the failings of the system in a single word: **politics**.

Earlier this year, Prime Minister Manmohan Singh gave a wide-ranging interview to the *McKinsey Quarterly*. He rated his own government's achievement as 6 out of 10, a performance he said was unsatisfactory. He acknowledged the need for better infrastructure, for more FDI, and also the need to move ahead in manufacturing. When asked whether the pace of implementation was fast enough, he replied:

> ... *economic policy and decision making do not function in a political vacuum. It takes a lot of time for us to take basic decisions. And furthermore, because we are a federal set-up, there are a lot of things that the central government does, but there are many things, like getting land, getting water, getting electricity — in all these matters the state government comes in, the local authority comes in. ... I do recognize that at times it gives our system the label that it is slow moving. In a world in which technology is changing at such a fast pace, where demand conditions change very fast, we need to look at a more innovative mechanism to cut down on this rigmarole of many tiers of decision-making processes.*

Prime Minister Singh added, "We are a coalition government and that limits our options in some ways."

Politics is a fact of life in any country. And coalition politics is a fact of Indian political life.

It has been suggested that India's slow growth is the consequence of its democratic system of government. Almost 40 years ago, Professor Jagdish Bhagwati wrote that India may face a "cruel choice between rapid expansion and democratic processes".

But democracy should not be made an alibi for inertia. There are many examples of authoritarian governments whose economies have failed. There are as many examples of democratic governments who have achieved superior economic performance. The real issue is whether any country's political system, irrespective of whether it is democratic or authoritarian, can forge a consensus on the policies needed for the economy to grow and create jobs for all, and can ensure that these basic policies are implemented consistently without large leakage. India's elite in politics, the media, the academia and think tanks can redefine the issues and recast the political debate. They should, for instance, insist on the provision of a much higher standard of municipal services.

By way of example, Chinese politics have always been plagued by factionalism. China also has great regional diversity. Like India, China also has powerful vested bureaucratic interests. But Deng Xiaoping forged a basic consensus among all political factions and the bureaucracy on the economic development and the necessary opening up to the outside world to succeed. A similar consensus can be achieved in India.

The passage of the Special Economic Zone (SEZ) Bill by the Lok Sabha (Lower House of the Indian Parliament) in May this year was an important move. SEZs can finesse some difficult internal issues blocking liberalization. Singapore has some experience with SEZs in China. If India thinks it useful, we are willing to share our experiences with you, building upon what we have done in the Bangalore International Technology Park. I must conclude with a word of caution. SEZs, once embarked upon, must be made to succeed, which means total and sustained commitment from politicians and bureaucrats at national, state and local levels. When they succeed, they will have a powerful effect on the whole economy, give a boost of confidence and spark off a healthy competitive dynamic between different states and regions. Successful SEZs will also erode opposition to reforms because their benefits become self-evident, as has happened in China.

A few months ago, in August, the communist Chief Minister of West Bengal was in Singapore to drum up investments for his state, offering market incentives to attract investors. He said: "The lesson from the collapse of the Soviet Union and from China is that [India] must reform, perform or perish." That very same month, members of his own party in Lok Sabha in New Delhi forced a retreat on India's privatization program. This is India's party politics.

Imponderables

There are some imponderables. American commentators believe that China's political system is too rigid, that it does not have the flexibility of pluralistic politics and democracy with freedom of speech, the media, assembly and respect for human rights. So China will encounter severe problems and setbacks. Professor Pranab Bardhan[1] of University of California, Berkeley, has explained the problem this way:

> *China's authoritarian system of government will likely be a major economic liability in the long run, regardless of its immediate implications for short-run policy decisions.*
>
> *But inequalities (particularly rural-urban) have been increasing in China, and those left behind are getting restive. With massive layoffs in the rust-belt provinces, arbitrary local levies on farmers, pervasive official corruption, and toxic industrial dumping, many in the countryside are highly agitated.*
>
> *China is far behind India in the ability to politically manage conflicts, and this may prove to be China's Achilles' Heel. Over the last fifty years, India's extremely heterogeneous society has been riddled with various kinds of conflicts, but the system has by and large managed these conflicts and kept them within*

---

[1] Pranab Bardhan is Professor of Economics at the University of California, Berkeley, and co-chair of the MacArthur Foundation-funded Network on the Effects of Inequality on Economic Performance, and Chief Editor of the *Journal of Development Economics*.

moderate bounds. For many centuries, the homogenizing tradition of Chinese high culture, language, and bureaucracy has not given much scope to pluralism and diversity, and a centralizing, authoritarian Communist Party has carried on with this tradition.

If they are right, India will draw ahead in the longer term.

Such analyses assume that the Chinese political system will remain static. If China's political structures do not adjust to accommodate the changes in its society resulting from high rates of growth, India will have an advantage because of its more flexible political system in the longer term.

But Bardhan also cautions: "India's reform has been halting and hesitant. India's heterogeneous society has been riddled with conflicts, but the system has by and large managed these. There are many severe pitfalls and roadblocks which India and China have to overcome."

Both India and China are huge countries with vast populations and long histories. They have to evolve standards of governance that are consonant with their cultures and the spirit of their civilizations.

Conclusion

At stake is the future of one billion Indians. India must make up for much time lost. There is in fact already a strong political consensus between India's two major parties that India needs to liberalize its economy and engage with the dynamic economies of the world. The BJP-led coalition government of former PM Atal Behari Vajpayee continued and indeed extended the economic liberalization policies of Manmohan Singh when he was Finance Minister in PM Narashima Rao's government. India now has a strong, able and experienced team with Manmohan Singh as PM. The time has come for India's next tryst with destiny.

Bibliography

Acharya, Amitav, "Realism, Institutionalism and the Asian Economic Crisis", *Contemporary Southeast Asia*, vol. 21, no. 1, April 1999, pp. 1–29.

———, *The Quest for Identity: International Relations of Southeast Asia*, Singapore, Oxford University Press, 2000.

———, "Clash of Civilizations? No, of National Interests and Principles", *International Herald Tribune*, January 10, 2001.

———, *Constructing a Security Community in Southeast Asia: ASEAN and the Problem of Regional Order*, London and New York, Routledge, 2001.

———, "Do Norms and Identity Matter? Community and Power in Southeast Asia's Regional Order", *Pacific Review*, vol. 18, no. 1, March 2005, pp. 95–118.

———, "Challenges for an Asean Charter", *The Straits Times*, October 24, 2005.

———, "East Asian Integration is Test for Big Powers", *Financial Times*, December 13, 2005.

Agence France Presse, "Singapore Ups Spending for Defence, Homeland Security", February 28, 2003, http://www.singapore-window.org/sw03/030228a1.htm.

———, "Singapore: Support for US Makes it Top Terror Target", May 24, 2003.

———, "Singapore Defends Support for War on Iraq, Says Weapons Search Not Over", June 11, 2003.

Alagappa, Muthiah, *The National Security of a Developing State: Lessons from Thailand*, Dover, Massachusetts, Auburn House, 1987.

Ariff, Mohamed & Hill, Hal, *Export-Oriented Industrialisation: The ASEAN ASEAN*, Sydney & Boston, Allen & Unwin, 1985.

ASEAN, "2001 ASEAN Declaration on Joint Action to Counter Terrorism", Bandar Seri Begawan, Brunei, November 5, 2001, http://www.aseansec.org.

————, "Report of the ARF Inter-Sessional Meeting on Counter-Terrorism and Transnational Crime", Karambunai, Sabah, Malaysia, March 21–22, 2003, http://www.aseansec.org/15133.htm.

Asian Development Bank, "Key Indicators of Developing Asian and Pacific Countries", Manila, 1990.

————, "Asian Development Outlook, Asian Development Bank", 1991.

Asian Political News, "Koizumi, Goh Agree on U.N. Role in Postwar Iraq", March 31, 2003, http://www.findarticles.com/cf_dls/m0WDQ/2003_March_31/99448274/p1/article.jhtml.

Ayoob, Mohammed, ed., *Regional Security in the Third World: Case Studies from Southeast Asia and the Middle East*, London, Croom Helm, 1986.

Azar, Edward E. & Moon, Chung-in, eds., *National Security in the Third World: The Management of Internal and External Threats*, Sydney, Edward Elgar, Aldershot, Allen & Unwin, 1988.

Balassa, Bela & Balassa, Carol, "Industrial Protection in the Developed Countries", *The World Economy*, vol. 7, June 1984, pp. 179–196.

Buszynski, Leszek, "Singapore: A Foreign Policy of Survival", *Asian Thought and Society*, July 29, 1985, pp. 128–136.

Buzan, Barry, *People, States and Fear*, 2nd ed., London, Harvester Wheatsheaf, 1991.

Chan, Heng Chee, *Singapore: The Politics of Survival: 1965–1967*, Singapore, Oxford University Press, 1971.

Chan, Heng Chee & ul Haq, Obaid, eds., *S. Rajaratnam: The Prophetic and the Political*, Singapore, Brash, Graham, 1987.

Chin, Kin Wah, ed., *Defence Spending in Southeast Asia*, Singapore, Institute of Southeast Asian Studies, 1987.

da Cunha, Derek, "Major Asian Powers and the Development of the Singaporean and Malaysian Armed Forces", *Contemporary Southeast Asia*, vol. 13, no. 1, 1991, pp. 57–71.

de Borchgrave, Arnuad, Interview with Lee Kuan Yew, May 15, 2001, http://app.mfa.gov.sg/.

Development Bank of Singapore, "US Trade Protectionism — Implications for Singapore and other NICs", Report no. 13, Singapore, 1987.

Dhanabalan, S., Text of a talk at the National University of Singapore Forum, November 27, 1981.

East, Maurice A., "Size and Foreign Policy", *World Politics*, vol. 25, July 1973, pp. 556–576.

Economic Bulletin 1989, "An Integrated European Market in 1992: Implications for Singapore", vol. 18, March 1989, pp. 11–16.

Fitchett, Joseph, "Campaign Proves the Length of U.S. Military Arm", *International Herald Tribune*, November 19, 2001.

Ganesan, N., "Factors Affecting Singapore's Foreign Policy towards Malaysia", *Australian Journal of International Affairs*, vol. 45, no. 2, 1991, pp. 182–195.

———, "Singapore's Foreign Policy Terrain", *Asian Affairs: An American Review*, vol. 19, no. 2, 1992, pp. 67–79.

Goh, Chok Tong, Address before the Eighth Pacific Economic Cooperation Conference, Singapore, May 20–22, 1991.

———, Speech at Asia Society, May 7, 2003, http://www.asiasociety.org/speeches/tong03.html.

———, Speech at the Nomura Singapore Seminar, November 8, 2005.

Haacke, Jurgen, *ASEAN's Diplomatic and Security Culture*, London, RoutledgeCurzon, 2002.

Huxley, Tim, "Singapore and Malaysia: A Precarious Balance", *The Pacific Review*, vol. 4, no. 3, 1991, pp. 204–213.

Indorf, Hans H., *Impediments to Regionalism in Southeast Asia*, Singapore, Institute of Southeast Asian Studies, 1984.

International Monetary Fund, "International Financial Statistics", Washington DC, 1990.

Jayakumar, S., Remarks in Parliament on "Strategic Review in the World, Including the Situation in Iraq, and Asia-Pacific Region", March 14, 2003, http://www.mfa.gov.sg/iraq.html#Iraq.

Jorgensen-Dahl, Arnfinn, *Regional Organisation and Order in South-East Asia*, London, Macmillan, 1982.

Knorr, Klaus, *The Power of Nations: The Political Economy of International Relations*, New York, Basic Books, 1975.

Koh, Tommy, "East Asia and Europe have an Important Date", *International Herald Tribune*, October 19, 2001.

Koh, Tommy & Chang, Li Lin, eds., *The Little Red Dot: Reflections by Singapore's Diplomats*, Singapore, World Scientific, 2005.

Kraus, Willy & Lutkenhorst, Wilfried, *The Economic Development of the Pacific Basin*, New York, St Martin's Press, 1986.

Krause, Lawrence *et al.*, eds., *The Singapore Economy Reconsidered*, Singapore, Institute of Southeast Asian Studies, 1987.

Lau, Teik Soon, "Malaysia-Singapore Relations: Crisis of Adjustment, 1965–68", *Journal of Southeast Asian History*, vol. 10, March 1969, pp. 155–176.

Lee, Chung H. & Naya, Seiji, eds., *Trade and Investment in Services in the Asia-Pacific Region*, Boulder, Colorado, Westview Press, 1988.

Lee, Hsien Loong, Speech before the Indonesia Forum, Jakarta, July 11, 1990.

———, Address at Asean 100 Leadership Forum, September 28, 2005, http://www.mfa.gov.sg/internet/.

———, Address at the 3rd Asean Business and Investment Forum, December 11, 2005.

Lee, Kuan Yew, "Asia-Pacific Region in the New Geopolitical Context", Keynote Address at the Informal Gathering of the World Economic Leaders, February 1990.

———, Text of speech at a banquet hosted by the Lord Mayor of London, May 24, 1990.

———, "After Iraq", Address to the 2nd Shangri-La Dialogue, May 30–June 1, 2003, http://www.iiss.org/shangri-la-more.php?itemID=10.

———, Address to the LKY School of Public Policy, April 4, 2005.

———, "Lee Kuan Yew Reflects", *Time Asia*, December 5, 2005, http://www.time.com/time/asia/covers/501051212/lky_intvu.html.

Lee, Tsao Yuan, ed., *Singapore: The Year in Review*, Singapore, Times Academic Press for Institute of Policy Studies, 1992.

Leifer, Michael, *Indonesian Foreign Policy*, London, George Allen & Unwin, 1983.

———, *Singapore's Foreign Policy: Coping with Vulnerability*, London, Routledge, 2000.

Lim, Chong Yah *et al.*, *Policy Options for the Singapore Economy*, Singapore, McGraw-Hill, 1988.

Lippmann, Walter, *US Foreign Policy: The Sword of the Republic*, Boston, Little, Brown, 1943.

Luciani, G., "The Economic Content of Security", *Journal of Public Policy*, vol. 8, no. 2, 1988, pp. 151–174.

Mahbubani, Kishore, "Agenda Item 49: Question of Equitable Representation on and Increase in the Membership of the Security Council", http://app.internet.gov.sg/scripts/mfa/pr/read_content.asp?View,1087.

———, Speech on Road Maps and Road Blocks, November 19, 2001, http://app.internet.gov.sg/scripts/mfa/pr/read_content.asp?View,1119.

———, United Nations Security Council Informal Meeting on military action in Afghanistan, Dow Jones Interactive, http://ptg.djnr.com/.

Milner, R.S., "Singapore's Exit from Malaysia: The Consequences of Ambiguity", *Asian Survey*, vol. 9, no. 3, March 1966, pp. 175–184.

Ministry of Trade and Industry, Singapore, *The Singapore Economy: New Directions*, Report of the Economic Committee, 1986.

Morrison, Charles E. & Suhrke, Astri, *Strategies of Survival: The Foreign Policy Dilemmas of Smaller Asian States*, Brisbane, University of Queensland Press, 1978.

Morrison, James, "Embassy Row", *The Washington Times*, October 13, 2005.

Online Newshour, May 7, 2003, http://www.pbs.org/newshour/bb/asia/jan-june03/goh_05-07-03.html.

Quah, Jon S.T., Chan, Heng Chee & Seah, Chee Meow, eds., *Government and Politics of Singapore*, Singapore, Oxford University Press, 1987.

Rajaratnam, S., "Singapore: Global City", Address to the Singapore Press Club, February 6, 1972.

Ramesh, M., "Economic Globalization and Policy Choices: Singapore", *Governance*, vol. 8, no. 2, 1995, pp. 243–260.

Ricks, Thomas E., "High-Tech Successes Point to a Sea Change in U.S. Military Thinking", *International Herald Tribune*, December 3, 2001.

Rieger, Hans Christoph, "Regional Economic Co-operation in the Asia Pacific Region", *Asian-Pacific Economic Literature*, vol. 3, no. 2, 1989, pp. 5–33.

Rodan, Garry, ed., *Singapore Changes Guard: Social, Political and Economic Directions in the 1990s*, Sydney, Longman Cheshire, 1993.

Rosenau, James N., "The New Global Order: Understanding and Outcomes", Paper presented at the XVth World Congress of the International Political Science Association, Buenos Aires, 1991.

Scalapino, Robert, Jusuf, Wanandi & Han, Sung-Joo, eds., *Regional Dynamics: Security, Political and Economic Issues in the Asia-Pacific Region*, Jakarta, Centre for Strategic and International Studies, 1990.

Shinn, James, ed., *Weaving the Net: Conditional Engagement with China*, New York, Council on Foreign Relations, 1996.

Singh, Bilveer, *Singapore: Foreign Policy Imperatives of a Small State*, National University of Singapore, Centre for Advanced Studies, 1988.

———, "Singapore, Malaysia and Indonesia Triangular Defence Pact: Potentials and Perils", *Asia Defence Journal*, December 1990, pp. 4–6.

Singh, Hari & Naraynan, Suresh, "Changing Dimensions in Malaysian Politics: The Johor Bahru By-Election", *Asian Survey*, vol. 29, no. 5, 1990, pp. 514–529.

Smith, Anthony L., *Special Assessment: The Asia-Pacific and the United States 2004–2005*, Honolulu, Asia-Pacific Center for Security Studies, 2005.

States News Service, White House Press Statement, Transcript, July 12, 2005.

Suriyamongkol, Marjorie L., *Politics of ASEAN Economic Co-operation: The Case of ASEAN Industrial Projects*, Singapore, Oxford University Press, 1988.

Taipei Times, "Mahathir Doesn't Want Australia at East Asia Summit", December 8, 2005, http://www.taipeitimes.com/News/world/archives/2005/12/08/2003283497.

Tan, Lian Choo, "Singapore's Support for Action on Iraq Prompted by Wider Concerns", *The Straits Times*, Forum Pages, June 11, 2003.

Tan, Tarn How, "No Sign of Iraqi Weapons: How Now, Singapore?", *The Straits Times*, June 7, 2003.

Thayer, Carlyle A., "ASEAN Ten Plus Three: An Evolving East Asian Community?" *Comparative Connections*, 4th Quarter, 2000.

The Straits Times, "Moderate Muslims Know Goal in Iraq: PM Goh", March 29, 2003.

———, "S'pore Lays Out Plans to Beat Airline Terrorists", January 4, 2004, http://straitstimes.asia1.com.sg/topstories/story/0,4386,228460-1073339940,00.html.

Trout, B. Thomas & Harf, James E., eds., *National Security Affairs, Theoretical Perspectives and Contemporary Issues*, New Brunswick, NJ, Transaction Books, 1982.

USA Today, "Bush Talks Terror with Singapore Leaders", October 21, 2003, http://www.usatoday.com/news/world/2003-10-21-bush-asia-x.htm.

U.S. Department of State, http://usinfo.state.gov/topical/pol/terror/texts/03102107.htm.

von Geusau, Frans A.M. Alting & Pelkmans, Jacques, eds., *National Economic Security: Perceptions, Threats and Policies*, The Netherlands, John F. Kennedy Institute, Tilburg, 1982.

Wong, Kan Seng, "Continuity and Change in Singapore's Foreign Policy", Speech to the Singapore Press Club, November 15, 1988.

———, Text of speech at Defence Asia '89 Conference on "Towards Greater ASEAN Military Cooperation: Issues and Prospects", Singapore, March 24, 1989.

———, Statement at the Paris Conference on Cambodia, October 23, 1991.

World Bank, "World Development Report 1991: The Challenge of Development", Oxford, Oxford University Press, 1991.

Wurfel, David & Burton, Bruce, eds., *The Political Economy of Foreign Policy in Southeast Asia*, London, Macmillan, 1990.

Yeo, George, "S'pore a Free Port But Will Give No Quarter to Terrorism", *The Straits Times*, October 12, 2001.

———, Speech at the US Chamber of Commerce, April 28, 2003, http://app10.internet.gov.sg/scripts/mfa/pr/admin/ussfta_list_title_SG display.asp?View,15.

———, Address at the Global Leadership Forum in Kuala Lumpur, September 6, 2005, http://www.mfa.gov.sg/internet/.

Zhang, Qiyue, Statement on Singaporean Deputy Prime Minister Lee Hsien Loong's Visit to Taiwan, July 11, 2004, http://www.chinaembasseycanada.org/eng/xwfw/2510/2535/t142801.htm.

Others:

Chapter 1

Far Eastern Economic Review, November 16, 1989.

Far Eastern Economic Review, April 30, 1992, p. 53.

Ministry of Defense, Singapore, 1992, p. 46.

Ministry of Foreign Affairs, Singapore, 1992, p. 1.

The Business Times, January 12–13, 1991.

The Straits Times, October 2, 1992, p. 13.

The Straits Times, May 7, 1993.

The Straits Times, June 17, 1993.

Chapter 2

Far Eastern Economic Review, June 27, 1991.

Far Eastern Economic Review, Review Publishing, Hong Kong, 1991, p. 28.

Goh, Chok Tong, *The Straits Times*, March 5, 1991.

PEER, August 4, 1989.

PEER, December 13, 1990.

PEER, October 24, 1991.

Singh, "American Military Facilities in Singapore", p. 17.

The Economist, "Pocket World in Figures", London.

The Straits Times, April 17, 1986.

Chapter 3

http://www.singapore-window.org/sw00/001011af.htm.
The Business Times, April 25, 2001.
The Business Times, June 13, 2001.
The Business Times, September 20, 2001.
The Business Times, October 2, 2001.
The Business Times, November 6, 2001.
The Straits Times, April 4, 2001.
The Straits Times, May 14, 2001.
The Straits Times, July 26, 2001.
The Straits Times, September 13, 2001.
The Straits Times, October 1, 2001.
The Straits Times, October 6, 2001.
The Straits Times, October 11, 2001.
The Straits Times, October 22, 2001.
The Straits Times, October 24, 2001.
The Straits Times, November 5, 2001.

Chapter 4

Online Newshour, May 7, 2003, http://www.pbs.org/newshour/bb/asia/jan-june03/goh_05-07-03.html.

Chapter 5

Agence France Presse, August 19, 2005.
Agence France Presse, August 25, 2005.
Agence France Presse, October 17, 2005.
BBC Monitoring Service, July 13, 2005.
BBC Monitoring Service, December 11, 2005.
BBC Monitoring Service Asia-Pacific, June 30, 2005.
BBC Monitoring Service Asia-Pacific, December 30, 2005.
Channel News Asia, April 26, 2005.
Channel News Asia, June 29, 2005.
China Daily, August 25, 2005.
George Yeo, in Parliament, cited in *The Straits Times*, October 18, 2005.

Indian Business Insight, June 30, 2005.

Inside the Pentagon, July 14, 2005.

Lianhe Zaobao, October 7, 2005.

Reuters News, April 25, 2005.

Reuters News, April 26, 2005.

States News Service, July 12, 2005.

The Business Times, October 27, 2005.

The Hindu, January 19, 2005.

The Hindu, March 6, 2005.

The New Paper, July 15, 2005.

The Straits Times, May 18, 2005.

The Straits Times, October 18, 2005.

The Straits Times, November 17, 2005.

The Straits Times, December 5, 2005.

Xinhua News Agency, December 30, 2005.

Index